Living on Borrowed Time

Living on Borrowed Time

Conversations with Citlali Rovirosa-Madrazo

Zygmunt Bauman

polity

First published in 2010 by Polity Press
Reprinted 2010

Polity Press
65 Bridge Street
Cambridge CB2 1UR, UK

Polity Press
350 Main Street
Malden, MA 02148, USA

ISBN-13: 978-0-7456-4738-8   **1006582000**
ISBN-13: 978-0-7456-4739-5(pb)

A catalogue record for this book is available from the British Library.

Typeset in 11 on 13 pt Sabon
by Toppan Best-set Premedia Limited
Printed and bound in Great Britain by MPG Books Limited, Bodmin, Cornwall

The publisher has used its best endeavours to ensure that the URLs for external websites referred to in this book are correct and active at the time of going to press. However, the publisher has no responsibility for the websites and can make no guarantee that a site will remain live or that the content is or will remain appropriate.

Every effort has been made to trace all copyright holders, but if any have been inadvertently overlooked the publisher will be pleased to include any necessary credits in any subsequent reprint or edition.

For further information on Polity, visit our website:
www.politybooks.com

Contents

Introduction

The first great recession of the last century, following the 1929 stock market crash, resulted in rival political systems and institutions that shaped a polarized world, with antagonistic forces fighting to establish different visions of economic development and, indeed, different visions of hegemonic domination; only to throw us back into decay when another recession, originating in Wall Street, lashed with the force of a tsunami in 2008.

This time, however, more challenging and decisive factors that no other civilization had known before were brought into the equation: unprecedented environmental threats – with natural disasters attributed to climate change – unprecedented levels of world poverty and an increase in the numbers of 'surplus population'; extraordinary scientific and technological developments presenting our society with critical predicaments; and a decline in the moral and political systems that had given the institutions of modernity a degree of social cohesion and stability.

Based on the work of Zygmunt Bauman, this book considers in historical context the meaning of the first global financial crisis of our young century, establishing links and considering its causes, implications and some of the moral and political challenges ahead. What may be considered a 'final' passage in the decline of the political institutions of modernity is addressed in this book, which seeks to explore matters beyond the mere economic phenomena of the Wall Street crash.

Financial slumps occur in historical contexts, in specific economic, political and moral discursive formations. The two largest financial downturns to have taken place in the space of two centuries have been associated with the long drawn out transition from modernity and with major historical developments – from *fascism* and *totalitarianism* to *neoliberalism*, from the Holocaust, to the fall of the Berlin Wall, the decline of the *ethnocratic state* in Latin America[1] and the war in Iraq. Both recessions took place in the context of huge political, moral, technological and military developments, which cannot be understood without looking into the archives of history and the ideological and economic formations that produced them.

Crisis can present us with opportunities to both modify and reflect on our situation, opportunities to try to understand how we got to the place where we are now and what we can do, if at all, to change our direction. It can represent a genuine opportunity for the production of 'new knowledge' and the drawing of *new epistemological frontiers*, with implications for future lines of research and debate. If anything, this crisis should be a chance to step back and ask more questions, an occasion to review and challenge all our theoretical frameworks and explore some of our historical and mental caves with more appropriate analytical and epistemological tools, hoping that we can identify and learn from our historical candidness. It is not good enough to try to look at the immediate economic and financial causes and effects of the financial collapse of the autumn of 2008: a thorough check-up is in order; a review of the framework that shaped our approach to the economy, assessing at today's historical crossroads which institutions will survive, and which may indeed become redundant or 'extinct'.

The colossal crash of Wall Street in 2008, and the subsequent collapse of the banking sector were not going to signal the fall of capitalism, as Bauman sharply tells us in this book, and as the world leaders showed when they gathered at the G20 summit in Washington shortly after the Wall Street disaster and ratified their commitment to the dogma of the free market economy,[2] proceeding to transform the state into a gigantic insurance company issuing insurance policies for the banks and Wall Street. Indeed, as Bauman argues here, 'cooperation between state and market is, under capitalism, a rule; conflict between them, if it ever surfaces, is an exception', and the latest developments only confirmed this rule.

The global financial downturn of 2008 and the inability or unwillingness of governments to regulate the financial and banking sectors – a characteristic feature of what Bauman regards as *liquid times*, sprang recession upon us, sending us into uncharted territories. In early 2009, the International Labour Organization estimated that global unemployment could increase to a staggering 50 million. The World Bank, in its economic forecast for 2009,[3] sentenced about 53 million people in developing countries to remain poor because of the world economic slowdown; in its report for the first quarter of 2009, it was estimated that the food and fuel price increases of 2008 had pushed another 130–150 million people into poverty and the global crisis was likely to keep 46 million more people below the 'absolute poverty line of $1.25 per day'. By February 2009, the biggest economic stimulus in US history was passed by the US Congress and it was considered a victory for President Barack Obama less than a month after he took office. The first month of Barack Obama's presidency included a banking bail-out worth at least $1.5 trillion (£1.02 trillion).[4] But these numbers did not match the scale of the problem at a global level. In its February 2009 report the World Bank stated that the economic downturn would reverse many of the gains made in reducing poverty in developing countries. And in Britain alone, the picture was hardly better, as a report by the Joseph Rowntree Foundation showed when it indicated that 'although recession will not greatly affect child poverty numbers, it will worsen the profile of child poverty'. That report estimated that '2.3 million children in the UK alone will be in poverty by 2010, missing the 1.7 million target set in 1999.'[5] It was to be expected that the greatest casualties of the recession were bound to be the world's poorest, inside or outside the 'advanced economies': inevitably, the economic slump would undermine the plans agreed by the United Nations to reach the poverty reduction targets for 2015 set in the Millennium Development Goals back in 2000, at the UN Millennium Summit. Any progress towards reducing infant mortality, which could see 200,000–400,000 more children die a year if the crisis persists, would have to be delayed, as World Bank president, Robert Zoellick admitted. At the time this book was concluded, this was only the tip of the iceberg, with the International

Monetary Fund warning that the entire world would have an economic growth rate close to zero into 2009, and the UN Food and Agriculture Organization alerting that world hunger had reached 1.02 billion.[6]

All these figures represented the broad picture in rather conservative numbers – if one is prepared, that is, to accept cold statistics and cold numbers as the best means of measuring and quantifying human misery, and 'human waste', but, as our conversations in the book show, there is more to this than simply numbers. The economic downturn, along with the subsequent plans of governments around the world to *collectivize* private financial debt, also revealed intricate linguistic constructions and complex discursive developments. Thus, in recent times, the language of rights has changed: *citizens* have become 'customers'; passengers and hospital patients have become 'clients'; *poverty* has become criminalized – as Bauman shows throughout his work – and 'extreme poverty' has become a 'pathological condition' rather than a reflection of structural injustice – a 'pathological dysfunction' of those who are poor, rather than the structural dysfunction of an economic system that generates and reproduces inequality;[7] and, more recently, *recession* itself has become regarded as an issue of 'national security', in the new language deployed by the new US National Intelligence.[8]

These financial developments and the crisis of the economic orthodoxy of the late twentieth century occurred as part of historical processes – including the rise and fall of the postwar Keynesian welfare state, the rise and fall of the nation-state, and democracy, all of which Bauman has examined in depth in various publications[9] and revisited in our conversations. There are, in Bauman's view, many instances in which our perceptions of both the state and its reality have changed, 'leading the consumer markets to slip into the role vacated by the state', a phenomenon that has become clearer since President Ronald Reagan in the US and Prime Minister Margaret Thatcher in the UK imposed privatization and deregulation policies with catastrophic consequences worldwide, consequences which led up to the 2008 crash. Another example of these dramatic changes concerns the mutations of the welfare state: the defining purpose of the agencies created for dealing with poverty is no longer, says Bauman, keeping the poor in good shape. Indeed 'policing the poor' is the new task of the state agencies that run 'something like a ghetto without walls, a camp without barbed wire (though densely packed with watch towers)'. Such are some of the themes we address herein as we embark upon an open, frank and interdisciplinary exchange, giving depth to the latest developments, rather than isolating them in a narrow and reductionist economic perspective.

Who is Zygmunt Bauman?

Like many other intellectuals from Eastern Europe, Bauman suffered under Nazi persecution and his family was forced to migrate to the Soviet Union in 1939, after Poland was invaded by Nazi forces. Having later escaped Stalinism and having returned to his native Poland, where he took up a position at Warsaw University, he became a victim of anti-Semitic purges in 1968 and was forced to migrate again, finding, in Britain, his permanent home, which he has since shared with his wife, the writer Janina Bauman. In 1971 he became a professor at Leeds University, where the substantial bulk of his research was produced, with astonishing results, until he formally retired in 1990, producing a prolific number of publications since.

Bauman experienced the polarization of a world divided between two conflicting visions of the way to tackle recession. At one extreme, the free market economy, leading US President Franklin D. Roosevelt to create the conditions in the early twentieth century for securing the hegemonic position of the US in the world; at the other extreme, fascism and totalitarianism – addressed in Bauman's early work[10] – leading to Hitler's and Stalin's atrocities, which shocked the world into shame and outrage, and which Bauman has considered with extraordinary eloquence and erudition in a number of publications.[11] Few academics of prominence have lived through and reflected on the horrors of these atrocities and two recessions, with the major political historical developments occurring between them.

Zygmunt Bauman lived and worked in the aftermath of the first major recession of the last century. Reflecting on the big picture of the international financial and banking crisis at the dawn of the new century, he cautioned: 'The present-day "credit crunch" is not an outcome of the banks' failure; on the contrary it is *fruit of*

their outstanding success: Success in transforming a huge majority
of men and women, old and young, into a race of debtors.'
Bauman examined and understood the capitalist historical developments as few have done, which is why, in his reflection on the
current crisis, and the collapsing institutions around it, he warns:
'The present "credit crunch" does not signal the end of capitalism;
only the exhaustion of a successive grazing pasture . . .' But,
for Bauman, there is no looking back: communism remains in
Bauman's eyes 'a short cut to slavery'. There is more, however;
Western democracy, he suggests in this book, is also at stake.
If modern democracy was born out of the needs and ambitions
of a *society of producers*, and if the ideas of 'self-determination'
and 'self-government' were made to the measure of practices of
production, the big question, says Bauman, is whether such ideas
can survive the passage from a society of producers to one of
consumers.

Bauman's international reputation and growing influence across
the humanities have inspired, among many others, those who are
interested in 'epistemological transgression' and the Eurocentric
foundations of Western political thought.[12] While the writings of
Bauman have become increasingly more prominent in the last
decade, and his ideas have spread, the insights gained from these
conversations are also likely to have implications for future
research.

There are several areas in the social sciences that have been
addressed by Bauman; his writings on law,[13] a number of essays
and books on culture and art,[14] his analysis of modernity and
postmodernity, being classed by some as a breakthrough,[15] particularly *Modernity and the Holocaust* (1989), but also his writings on ethics,[16] *Postmodernity and its Discontents*,[17] *In Search of
Politics* (1999)[18] and, more recently, *Liquid Modernity* (2000).[19]

Bauman addresses some of the tragedies of our time that
unfolded as a result of economic globalization,[20] and the legacy
of 'human waste' and 'surplus population', as Bauman refers to
the millions of migrants, unemployed and vagabonds in a society
where humans are regarded as pariahs, only worthy of being seen
as waste material. Society, says Bauman, 'can only be raised to the
level of community as long as it effectively protects its members
against the horrors of misery and indignity; that is, against the
terrors of being excluded [and] being condemned to "social redun-

dancy" and otherwise consigned to [being] "human waste" '.[21] But it is not only the 'pariahs' who are part of the saga of 'surplus population' and 'human waste' – an issue we address in our conversations; the truth is, as Bauman suggests here, borrowing from Ehrlich's views on population: 'there are in fact too many rich people.'[22]

Bauman's innovative notion of *liquidity* is a metaphor to describe the notable social and political transformations in the mid and late twentieth century, represented by the disintegration or 'liquidation' of the institutions of modernity. In his framework, liquid modernity is 'post-Utopian', 'post-Fordist', 'post-National', and 'post-panoptical'.[23] Neoliberalism – both cause and effect of the nation-state crisis – played a decisive role, in Bauman's view, in the latest transitions of liquid capitalism, one of its features being 'the passage from a society of producers into a society of consumers', with the distinctive and dramatic addition of a transmutation into 'a race of debtors'; and with the new lamentable role of the state as 'an executor of market sovereignty'[24] in which 'the radical privatization of human fate goes along and apace with the radical deregulation of industry and finances'.[25]

In Bauman's view, our socially constructed communities, identities and institutions have become increasingly more precarious and more elusive,[26] giving way to 'liquid identities' in a world where the decline of the state and the blurring of national borders are irreversible.[27] 'Liquid times' also produced, in Bauman's framework, a discourse where the culture of citizens' rights (traditionally belonging to the welfare state and discourses of modernity) is downgraded into 'a culture of charity, humiliation and stigma',[28] a theme debated further in this book.

We learn from Bauman that *identity*, including gender identity, has a provisional and elusive nature;[29] this is probably the reason why orthodox feminism has not found fertile ground in his work, with only a few of the academics concerned with *feminist* theory having considered his writings.[30] But, most importantly, *identity* and *otherness* have become irrelevant in the sociological framework of the Polish author because, as Ilan Semo puts it, in Bauman's work *Difference* (singular, with a capital D) has evaporated like a mirage; there are only *differences* (plural, with a small d) and they change continuously.[31] This is also the reason why Bauman rejects Charles Taylor and other advocates of 'fashionable multiculturalism'.[32] In his view, perceiving 'identity and the nature of culture as like things, complete inside and clearly delineated on the outside' is a mistake.[33] However, his thoughts on identity take another turn in this book as we discuss the implications for the very meaning of humanity in the age of biotechnology and the latter's deployment of so-called 'post-humanity'.

In Bauman's later writing, 'liquid cities' whose citizens have been transformed into armies of consumers, are no longer 'cosmopolis' but fortress-like 'cities of fear'.[34] They confront us with the reality that we have become obsessed with security to the extent that we have 'normalized the state of emergency',[35] with the paradoxical result that borders between the state and civil society have also become blurred. Thus today's 'plot of fear' is no longer found only in the prospect of the state devouring a society (by means of a dictatorship), or in the society erupting in the state (by means of mass revolution), but in the very act of becoming the excluded and marginalized.[36] As Semo explains, in Bauman's analysis, governments today do not focus on the ability to produce consensus (cf. Gramsci) but on the cunning involved in restoring the motives of fear. Bauman again: 'if it were not for people fearing, it would be difficult to imagine the need for a state' . . . the state is a 'fear-management, fear-shuffling and fear-recycling plant'.

Bauman is in debt to Lyotard[37] as he is to Derrida.[38] Like them, he realizes the need to abandon the illusion of all grand narratives, including those regarding the 'elusive universality'.[39] Lyotard's *The Postmodern Condition* (1984) is present in Bauman's early work, including *Legislators and Interpreters* (1987), where Bauman, in line with other authors concerned with legal deconstruction,[40] insists that we live in an age of 'competing interpretations'. Thus the shift away from 'foundationalism', and the distancing from metanarratives, is not only a symptom of 'liquid times', but could, in fact, in a paradoxical way, be a healthy approach to understanding the *autopoietic* circle of law[41] and other tautological constructions. However, Bauman is critical of those who 'celebrate' postmodernity as a clear landmark beyond modernity, and warns of the risks of making postmodernity a grand narrative itself.

Another key concept gathered from reading Bauman's work, both in his early period[42] and in more recent times,[43] seems to be that of utopia. But as M. Jacobsen and R. Jacoby before him have pointed out,[44] utopia has been neglected, when it has not been abandoned, by intellectuals and academics on the left. Utopia is in disrepute and one of the reasons for this, according to Bauman, is its stubborn link to modernity; thus in our conversations he remarks: 'it is only the pioneers of modernity who needed utopian images to drive them . . . "Teleology" is primarily a modern notion.' But in his early work he had written: 'The driving force behind the search for utopia is neither the theoretical nor the practical reason, neither cognitive, nor the moral interest, but the principle of hope.'[45] And he has not parted from this vision altogether, as our discussion here shows. Distancing from modernity does not necessarily mean giving up utopia, in the sense of hopefulness, in Bauman's writings. Drawing on the work of French philosopher Emmanuel Levinas,[46] and his crucial notion of *being for the Other*, Bauman allows room for suggesting that *otherness* could play a part in utopia in the sense of hope – though he never really seems fully to subscribe to Levinas's yearnings.[47] In fact, more recently he has warned: '*the Other* may be a promise, but it is also a threat',[48] and he remains rather 'suspicious' of communitarian politics.[49] Ilan Semo puts it like this: 'if identity in Bauman is temporary substance, *the Other* is nothing but an invention, an anthropological construction inevitably anchored in some kind of ethnocentrism'.[50]

When, over a decade ago, Bauman had placed himself within the postmodern tradition ('postmodernity, one may say, is modernity without the illusions')[51] – a position he later abandoned in favour of the concept of 'liquidity' – ('modernity is refusing to accept its own truth')[52] – he was, in fact, anticipating more efficient epistemological tools to examine neoliberalism. At his age, Bauman's unyielding and prolific pen refuses to accept any possibility of surrendering in his battle against time, which, in many ways, is the race against the 'loose demons of economic globalization',[53] the creatures of neoliberalism and the stubborn remains of totalitarianism and fascism encompassed in this book.

Why Zygmunt Bauman?

If one could compare social theories or sociological theoretical thinkers to kitchen equipment, Zygmunt Bauman would be, without doubt, one of the sharpest knives. Like most blades, however, his knife is doubled edged. Try mastering its use without cutting yourself and you will always end up with a sliced finger dripping red all over the onions – you never get to their core because there simply isn't one. French structuralists[54] and the Polish author have that in common: they can make the intricate layers of history and the saga of Western philosophy look like layered onions.

Bauman challenges communism as he challenges capitalism – perhaps another good reason for reading his work in times of recession. Bauman rebels against the church and Bauman rebels against the state – 'the inseparable Siamese twins', as he likes to call them – showing no signs of yearning for either.

And as if that was not enough, he also seems defiant about science – or, more precisely, while he retains his trust and respect for it, he appears to be suspicious of its love affair with the market. In many ways 'liquid capitalism' seems to have managed to put science at the service of profit, so 'rebelling' is not out of order. Though Bauman knows where he stands epistemologically ('Popper solved that issue for me, pointing out that the amazing creative potential of science lies in its power of refutation, not in the power of its proofs'),[55] he also appears to be alerting us to the paradoxes of science and technology in the same spirit as Georg Simmel – who influenced him greatly – last century: inevitably 'the control over nature which technology offers us is paid for by our enslavement to it'.[56] Thus signs of paradigmatic crisis are not confined to the realm of the political state and its 'wobbly institutions'; they appear to reach as far as our perceptions of the scientific institutions. Here our conversations suggest that a new debate and new research are needed on the relationship between the humanities and the scientific institutions, particularly the biological sciences,[57] because the problem of economic deregulation has also, in many ways, affected the scientific community. In fact, one thing that we learnt from the 2008 crisis was that we now seem to 'owe' the last bastion of our humanity, and indeed its very name and dignity, to powerful emerging industries: genetic engineering and biotechnology's new commodities such as DNA decoding, genome patenting and their 'post-human', 'trans-human' 'neo-human' market.[58] As in the case of the financial market, in the genetics market certain experimental procedures do not seem to have been closely regulated, in spite of existing and compelling guidelines and recommendations by the international community.[59] The reach of the existing regulatory bodies tends to extend only to publicly funded research, leaving the private sector largely unregulated. It is not for nothing that biotechnology-related companies shine out from Wall Street's electronic listings, with nearly 25 per cent of Wall Street shares allegedly belonging to biotechnology companies, as Spanish biologist M. S. Dominguez[60] notes: biotechnology is not just another industry and, when underregulated, there is a potential risk of undermining the extraordinary achievements in medical and scientific research and overshadowing science's historical role – notwithstanding which, Bauman has not fully lost faith in it. But, as Bauman notes in this book, 'Engineering human affairs is not, of course, the genomists' invention. The intention to engineer (indeed create "new man") accompanied the modern order from its inception)' and, as Bauman seems to be suggesting in our conversations, this is one of the biggest challenges of our times. But the question as to whether or not it is time to speak of 'liquid science' is open to future debate.

As for Bauman's perception of the church and the state, the 'historical twins', prospects are grim: the state and the church have something in common, their power to exploit and their ability to act as *fear managers*, as Bauman avers in this publication. Big Brother – the 'secular eye' that watches over us, just as the religious eye once did (and still does) – has grown into a robust surveillance industry, both competing against and supporting the weakening state in its role as a 'fear manager'.[61] Fear management is a card played well by both the state and religion and it is imperative that we should understand the rules of this game if we want to gain perspective in our perception of society today; Bauman's analytical approach allows us to do this.

In a very paradoxical sense, moral responsibility is Bauman's sole motive for writing: he is a non-religious man who writes for an ethical reader, a social thinker who dismisses the idea of a supranatural being, and yet a man whose compassion, moral integrity and moral commitment to humanity would provoke the envy of any dogmatic, religious or secular man. Any reader of faith who is ready for an honest confrontation will benefit from reading Zygmunt Bauman because there is, in a paradoxical way, a language of profound compassion. Likewise, readers of strong political affiliations and dogmatic views must brace themselves for a painful confrontation with the walls and fortifications of history. This is precisely the kind of exercise we need to be able to understand if we are to grasp what has happened in the economic arena in recent times.

Both reading and conversing with Bauman is highly addictive, not least because of his elegant sense of humour and irony. Debating with him, however, is like entering a dark cave with him, and losing him within seconds, realizing that he has taken different tunnels and realizing that there are no visible beams of light at the tunnel's edge, no clear-cut paths to follow – resort to humour if you can, otherwise settle for crying. Bauman invites us to read history, law, economics, culture and politics from a different perspective, conveys an understanding of the painfulness of the journey, and reminds us that we are not the sole victims of today's financial crisis, created by capitalism and those wedded to it. It is uncertain whether in the era of President Obama, and the aftermath of the global financial crisis of 2008, our societies – trapped by the illusions of economic globalization, and often portrayed in this book with Rosa Luxemburg's celebrated metaphor of a 'snake devouring itself' – will finally perish. It will, subsequently be revealed whether or not our attitudes to nature and our attitudes to our own species can change: will the self-devouring snake plunge its sharp fangs into our own children and our only planet, before it finally goes for the head? The answer may, perhaps, lie in every one of us, in our ability to challenge Bauman's 'liquid creatures' and our ability and desire to search for our true humanity, as the Polish author exhorts us to do in his compelling writings.

Citlali Rovirosa-Madrazo

Part One

Conversation I

The credit crunch:
an outcome of the Bank's failure,
or a fruit of its outstanding success?
Capitalism is not dead

Citlali Rovirosa-Madrazo *You grew up during the first major recession of the twentieth century and experienced extraordinary historical times in its aftermath. You have since come a long way, only to find yourself amidst the first major recession of the twenty-first century. But you were never a mere passive observer of what 'history threw at' you; from a very young age you were politically active and engaged in controversial movements deeply resonant of today's new challenges. What were your first thoughts in the last few weeks when you realized that we were facing a 'financial tsunami' and were heading towards the 'implacable collapse' of the Western economy? What could we have learnt from the twentieth century recession and failed to learn? What can we still learn from the mistakes made in the past? Did you experience a socialist or indeed a communist nostalgia?*

Zygmunt Bauman 'Communist nostalgia' is for me out of the question. Communism, which I once described as 'socialism's impatient younger brother', means to me a project of an enforced 'shortcut to the Kingdom of Freedom' – which, however attractive and emboldening it may sound in words, proves in its practical application to be a shortcut to the cemetery of liberties, and to slavery, whenever it is executed. The idea of shortcuts, not to mention the practice of enforcement, stands in stark opposition to liberty. Enforcement is a self-propelling and self-intensifying practice; once started, it must focus on a vigilant and never slackening effort to keep the enforced meek and silent. If it is proclaimed in the name of human freedom (as Jean-Jacques Rousseau once mused it could be, as Lenin resolved to hammer home, and as Albert Camus saw in despair was the fast settling habit of the twentieth century), it destroys its declared target and then it has nothing to serve except its own continuity.

'Socialist nostalgia'? It would be, if I had ever abandoned my belief in the wisdom and humanity of the socialist stance (which I have not), and it could be, if I did not perceive 'socialism' as a stance, an attitude, a guiding principle, but viewed it as a type of society, a specific design and a particular model of social order (which I have not for a long time now). Socialism means to me a heightened sensitivity to inequality and injustice, oppression and discrimination, humiliation and the denial of human dignity. To take a 'socialist stance' means opposing and resisting all those outrages whenever and wherever they occur, in whatever name they are perpetrated and whoever their victims are.

And 'capitalism'? As the recent 'financial tsunami', as you have vividly called it, has shown 'beyond reasonable doubt' to the millions of those who were lulled by the mirage of 'prosperity now and forever' into believing in capitalist markets and capitalist banking as the patent methods of successful problem-resolution – capitalism is at its best when creating problems, not when trying (if it does!) to resolve them. Capitalism, as with systems of natural numbers in Kurt Gödel's famous theorem, cannot be simultaneously consistent and complete; if it is consistent with its own principles, problems arise it cannot tackle; and if it tries to resolve them, it cannot do that without falling into inconsistency with its own founding assumptions.

Long before Gödel worked out and jotted down his theorem, Rosa Luxemburg wrote her 'capitalist accumulation' study, in which she suggested that capitalism cannot survive without 'non-capitalist' or 'pre-capitalist' economies; it can proceed according to its principles as long as there are 'virgin lands' as yet untouched and open for expansion and exploitation – yet, when it conquers them for the purpose of exploitation disguised as cultivation, capitalism deprives them of their pre-capitalist virginity and so reduces the supply of its own future nourishment. Capitalism, to put it bluntly, is essentially a parasitic system. Like all parasites, it may thrive for a time once it finds an as yet unexploited organism on which it can feed, but it can't do that without harming the host and sooner or later destroying thereby the conditions of its prosperity, or even of its own survival. Writing in an era of rampant imperialism and territorial conquest, Rosa Luxemburg did not and could not, however, foresee that the premodern lands of exotic continents are not the only potential 'hosts' on which capitalism can feed to prolong its lifespan and initiate successive time-stretches of prosperity. Now, a hundred years later, we have come to know that capitalism's strength lies in its amazing ingenuity in seeking and finding (or indeed producing) new species of hosts whenever the previously exploited species get thin on the ground or are extinguished; we came to know, too, the virus-like expediency and speed with which it manages to readjust to the idiosyncrasies of its new grazing pastures. The present 'credit crunch' does not signal the end of capitalism – only the exhaustion of the latest grazing pasture.

There was once a joke about two salesmen travelling to Africa on behalf of their respective shoe companies. The first sent home a message: don't dispatch any shoes – everybody here walks barefoot. The message sent by the second was: dispatch 10 million pairs of shoes immediately – everybody here walks barefoot. That old joke was composed in praise of aggressive business acumen and in condemnation of the business philosophy prevalent at the time: of business aimed at the satisfaction of existing needs, and of offers following the current demand. In the few dozen years that followed, business philosophy completed its U-turn, however. Today, in a setting successfully transformed from one of a society of producers (profits made mostly from the exploitation of hired labour) into one of a society of consumers (profits made mostly from the exploitation of consumerist desires), the ruling business philosophy insists that the purpose of business is to prevent needs from being satisfied and to evoke, induce, conjure and beef up more needs clamouring for satisfaction and more potential customers prompted into action by such needs: in short, that the task of the offer is to create demand. That belief applies to all products – of factories or of financial companies alike. As far as business philosophy is concerned, loans are no exception: the offer of a loan must create and magnify the need for borrowing.

The introduction of credit cards was a signal of things to come. Credit cards were sprung 'on the market' a couple of dozen years ago under the telling and uniquely seductive slogan: 'take the waiting out of wanting'. You desire something but haven't earned enough money to pay its selling price? Well, in olden times, now fortunately over and gone, you would have to delay the satisfaction of the desire (that delay, according to Max Weber, one of the fathers of modern sociology, was the rule that made the advent of modern capitalism possible): you would have to tighten your belt, avoid many temptations and deny yourself many momentary joys, spend prudently and frugally, and put the monies you managed to spare that way in a savings book, hoping that with due care and patience you would collect enough of them to make your dreams come true. Thank God and the banks' benevolence, no longer! With a credit card, you can reverse the order: you can enjoy now, pay later! A credit card makes you free to manage your own satisfactions: to obtain things when you want them, not when you earn them and can afford them.

This was the promise. But there was also small print attached, difficult to decipher, even if easy to divine in a moment of reflection: that every 'later' would turn at some point into a 'now', and that the loans would then need to be repaid, and the repayment of the loans you took in order to take the waiting out of wanting and to promptly satisfy your current desires would make it all the more difficult to satisfy the desires of the future. Not thinking about 'later' meant in that case, as it always does, storing up trouble. One can stop worrying about the future only at one's peril. There will surely be a price to pay. What one will find out sooner rather than later is that the somewhat uncomfortable delay of satisfaction has been replaced by a brief delay of the truly terrifying punishment for haste. One may have the joy when one wants; but speeding its arrival won't make enjoyment more affordable. In the last account, only the realization of that sad truth will be delayed.

Toxic and sad as it may be, that was not the only small print surreptitiously attached to the promise in bold letters of 'enjoy now, pay later'. In order to avoid reducing the effect of credit cards and easy borrowing to just a one-off lender's profit, the debt incurred had to be and was bound to be transformed into a permanent profit-earning asset. You can't repay your debts? First of all, you shouldn't try to repay them in full and right away – having no debts is not at all the ideal state to be in. Secondly, don't worry: unlike the old-style niggardly moneylenders of yore, eager to have their loans promptly repaid at a time fixed in advance and not to be extended – we, the new race of generous and benevolent lenders, do not call back our money; instead, we offer to lend you yet more credit to repay the old debt, leaving you moreover with some extra money (that is, debt) to pay for new joys. We are the banks who like to say 'yes'. Your friendly banks. Smiling banks – as one of the most ingenious of commercial slogans declared.

What none of the advertisements openly declared, leaving the truth to the debtors' own dark premonitions, was that the lending banks don't really want their debtors to repay the loans. Were the debtors duly to repay their borrowings, they would no longer be in debt; but it is precisely their being in debt (and so paying interest month in, month out on their loans) that the new race of friendly (and remarkably ingenious) moneylenders have decided and managed to recast into the principal source of their continuous profit. Clients promptly returning the money they borrowed are the present-day moneylenders' nightmare. People refusing to spend money they did not earn and refraining from borrowing it are of no use to moneylenders – and neither are the people who (whether prompted by prudence or by old-fashioned honour) hasten to repay their debts on time.

For their and their shareholders' profits, banks and credit card providers now count on the continuous 'servicing' of debts, rather than on their prompt repayment. As far as they are concerned, an 'ideal borrower' is one who would never repay the loan in full. People with savings accounts but no credit cards are viewed as a challenge to marketing skills: 'virgin lands' yelling for profitable, promising rich new crops of exploitation. Once drawn under cultivation (that is, into the lending–borrowing game), they should never be allowed to opt out – to 'lie fallow' again. To keep them in the game, heavy penalties are imposed on those who wish to repay their mortgage loans in full before the scheduled time. Until the recent 'credit crash', banks and issuers of credit cards were more than willing to offer new loans to insolvent debtors to cover the unpaid interest on earlier loans. One of the major credit card companies in Britain recently caused a public outcry (short-lived, to be sure) when it let the pig out of the poke: when it refused to reissue cards to clients who repaid their debts in full every month, thereby avoiding interest just as the banks avoid paying taxes.

To sum up: the present-day 'credit crunch' is not an outcome of the banks' failure. On the contrary, it is a fully predictable, even if by and large not predicted, fruit of their outstanding success: success in transforming a huge majority of men and women, old and young, into a race of debtors. Banks got what they aimed to get: a permanent race of debtors, the condition of 'being in debt' made self-perpetuating, the universal habit of seeking more loans seen as the sole realistic (even if temporary) stay of execution.

Entering that condition has recently become easier than ever before in human history; escaping that condition has never been as difficult. Anyone who could be made into a debtor, including the uncountable millions who could not and should not have been lured into borrowing in the first place, has already been enticed and seduced into living on credit. As in all previous mutations of capitalism, this time, too, the state assisted the establishment of new grazing grounds for capitalist exploitation. It was on President Clinton's initiative that the 'subprime', government-sponsored mortgages in the US were introduced to offer credit for buying houses to people with no means to repay their loans – and so to transform into debtors parts of the population hitherto inaccessible to credit-mediated exploitation. But just as the disappearance of barefoot people spells trouble for the shoe industry, so the disappearance of debt-free people spells disaster for the loan industry. Rosa Luxemburg's famous surmise has been verified once more: again, capitalism came dangerously close to unwitting suicide by managing to exhaust all the reserves of new virgin lands for exploitation.

In the US, the average debt of a household has risen in the last eight years – the years of apparently unprecedented prosperity – by 22 per cent. The total sum of unpaid credit card loans increased by 15 per cent. And perhaps most menacingly, the overall debt of college students, the future political, economic and spiritual elite of the nation, doubled. Students have been forced/encouraged to live on credit – to spend money which at best they might hope to earn many years later (assuming the prosperity and consumerist orgy lasted that long). The training in the art of 'living in debt', and living in debt permanently, has been incorporated into the curriculum of national education. A very similar situation has

been reached in Great Britain. In August 2008, the total of un-
repaid consumer debts overtook the entire gross domestic product.
British households now owe more than the value of the whole
produce of their factories, farms and offices. The rest of European
countries are following suit, not far behind. The banker's planet
is running short of virgin land, the vast expanses of endemically
barren land having already been recklessly exploited.

CRM *Are the latest events in the economy going to represent a
turning point; the 'decisive moment' in Western political thought?
Have our political paradigms (modern or postmodern) also crum-
bled and vanished, never to return? Is it time to bury the dead?*

ZB The news of capitalism's death, as Mark Twain would have
said, are grossly exaggerated . . . Even the obituaries of the credit-
mediated phase in the history of capitalist accumulation are
premature.
   The reaction to the 'credit crunch' so far, impressive and even
revolutionary as it may appear once it has been recycled in the
media headlines and politicians' sound-bites, has been 'more of
the same' – in the vain hope that the potential of that particular
virgin land for profit and consumption reinvigoration has not yet
been fully exhausted: an effort to recapitalize the moneylenders
and to make their debtors creditworthy once more, so the business
of lending and borrowing, of falling in debt and staying there, can
return to the 'usual'. The welfare state for the rich (which, unlike
its namesake for the poor, has never had its rationality questioned,
let alone put out of operation) has been brought back to the
showrooms from the service quarters to which its offices were
temporarily relegated to avoid invidious comparisons. The state's
muscles, long unused for that purpose, have been publicly flexed
again – this time for the sake of continuing the game that makes
its muscle-flexing resented yet – abominably – unavoidable; a
game that curiously cannot bear the state flexing its muscles, yet
cannot survive without it.
   What is joyously (and foolishly) forgotten on that occasion is
that the nature of human suffering is determined by the way
humans live. The roots of the currently lamented pain, like the
roots of all social evil, are sunk deep in our contrived and trained
mode of life: by our carefully cultivated and by now deeply

entrenched habit of running for consumer credit whenever there is a problem to face or a difficulty to be overcome. Life on credit is addictive like few if any other drug, and surely still more addictive than other tranquillizers on offer, and decades of lavish supply of a drug cannot but lead to a shock and a trauma whenever the supply runs thin or even grinds to a halt. We are now advised to take the apparently easy way out of shock that afflicts both drug addicts and drug pushers: through resuming the (hopefully regular) supply of drugs. Back to the addiction that seemed until now to help us all so effectively not to worry too much about problems, and even less about their roots.

Reaching to the root of the problem that has now been taken out of the 'top secret' compartment and brought into the focus of public attention is not – can't be – an instant solution. It is, however, the only solution with a chance of being adequate to the enormity of the problem; and of surviving the intense, yet comparatively brief agonies of withdrawal.

Thus far, there are not many signs that we've arrived anywhere near the root of the problem. The moment it was halted at the edge of a precipice by a lavish injection of 'taxpayers' money', TSB Lloyds bank started lobbying the Treasury to divert part of the rescue package to shareholders' dividends; notwithstanding the official indignation of state spokespersons, it proceeded undisturbed to pay bonuses to those whose intemperate greed had brought the disaster on the banks and their clients. We have heard from the US that $70 billion, about 10 per cent of the subsidies the federal authorities intend to pump into the American banking system, have been used to pay bonuses to the people who brought that system close to ruin. Since then, that practice has become so repetitive that it no longer hits the headlines. However impressive the measures already undertaken by governments, intended or declared, they are all aimed at 'recapitalizing' the banks and enabling them to return to 'normal business': in other words, to the activity that bears the main responsibility for the present crisis. If borrowers have failed to pay directly and personally the interest on past consumer orgies inspired and beefed up by the banks, perhaps they may be induced/forced to pay the cost via taxes raised by the state.

We have not as yet started to give serious thought to the sustainability of our consumer-and-credit-propelled society. A 'return to normality' portends return to bad, and always potentially dangerous, ways. The intention to do so is worrying: it signals that neither the people who run the financial institutions nor our governments have reached to the root of the trouble in their diagnoses – let alone in their deeds. Quoting Hector Sants, the head of the Financial Services Authority, who had confessed a few days earlier to 'business models ill-equipped to survive the stress . . . a fact that we regret', Simon Jenkins, the uniquely insightful analyst of the *Guardian*, observed that 'it was like a pilot protesting that his plane was flying just fine except for the engines'. But Jenkins did not lose hope: he still reckoned that once the culture of 'greed is good' had been 'tested to destruction by the recent hysteria of City incomes', the 'non-economic components of what we vaguely refer to as good life will take more prominence'; both in our life philosophy, and our government's political strategy. Let us hope with him: we haven't yet reached the point of no return, there is still time (however short) to reflect and change track, we may yet turn that shock and that trauma to our and our children's advantage.

CRM *In the weeks following the financial crisis, at the time of putting these conversations down on paper, the state appeared to have completed a mutation into a gigantic insurance company, issuing insurance policies for the banks and Wall Street, as North American author Naomi Klein put it in one of her articles in* The Nation. *Is this transmutation going to mark the decisive point, the colossal collapse of a discursive formation that had somehow managed to survive liquid times?*

ZB A sort of 'welfare state' for the rich (or, more exactly, the policy of the mobilization by the state of those public resources that private or public companies have been unable to seduce the public into handing over) is in no way a novelty – only its scale and public exposure have made it dramatic enough to cause an outcry. According to Stephen Sliwinski of the Cato Institute, even in 2006 the federal government of the US spent $92 billion subsidizing such giants of American industry as Boeing, IBM or General Motors.

Many years ago, in a book called *Legitimation Crisis*, Jürgen Habermas suggested that the state is 'capitalist' in as far as its prime function and indeed raison d'être is 'recommodification' of capital and labour. The substance of capitalism, Habermas reminded us, is the meeting of capital and labour. The purpose of that meeting is a commercial transaction: capital buys labour. For that transaction to take place, two conditions must be met: capital must be able to buy, and labour must be 'sellable' – attractive enough for capital to do the buying. The main task (and indeed the 'legitimation') of the capitalist state is seeing to it that both conditions are met. The state must therefore do two things. First, subsidize capital in case it is short of the money that the purchase of labour requires. And second: to ensure that the labour available for purchase is worth purchasing: that it is able to endure the strains of the factory floor, being bodily strong and in good health, adequately fed, and properly trained in the skills and behavioural habits indispensable in industrial employment. Without a state-administered subsidy, prospective capitalist employers could hardly afford all that expenditure; carrying them would make the cost of hiring labour exorbitant by their standards.

Habermas wrote all that at the twilight of the 'solid modern' society of producers – and he interpreted (wrongly, as it has since transpired) the obvious failure of states to fulfil the two tasks which that society needed to survive as the 'legitimation crisis' of the capitalist state. What was happening in fact, however, was a transition from the 'solid' modern society of producers to the 'liquid' modern society of consumers. The prime source of capitalist accumulation moved from industry to the consumer market. To keep capitalism alive, it was no longer the 'recommodification' of capital and labour to make the transaction of buying–selling labour possible that was the prime requisite; what was sorely needed instead to keep capitalism going were rather state subsidies to render capital able to sell commodities, and consumers able to buy them. Credit was the magic contraption expected and hoped to perform that double task; and we can say now that in the liquid phase of modernity the state is 'capitalist' in as far as it assures the continuous availability of credit and the continuous ability of consumers to obtain it.

CRM *You experienced the initial phases of the transition from an economy based on industrial capital to one based on financial capital. Indeed, such a transition is one of the many subjects in your academic work. You also lived through extraordinary histori-*

cal episodes, including a dramatic clash between totalitarianism and liberalism. The world then, as now, seemed at a crossroad, it seemed to be faced with an apparent 'dilemma': a 'dictatorship of the state' or a 'dictatorship of the market' (the latter never having been called this before by any Western leader – until, that is, French president Nicolas Sarkozy proclaimed its death in the aftermath of the collapse of Wall Street). Were those real dilemmas about incompatible political and economic systems, or perhaps a reflection of our typical binary schizophrenic thinking, our human inability to think outside dichotomies? Or were they (and are they still) a mere reflection of the will to gain power and a desire for domination?

ZB When elephants fight, pity the grass . . . In the war between the two pretenders to dictatorship you've named, the fate of the poor, the indolent and those otherwise unable to achieve the conditions of physical and social survival was all but forgotten (in deed if not in words). But presenting the two dictatorships as the major opposition and dilemma of contemporary society is profoundly misleading; one can easily take appearances for realities and declarations for policies . . .

First of all, let us point out that the two elephants, the state and the market, might have been occasionally in battle, but their normal and ordinary, indeed routine, relationship under capitalism was that of symbiosis. Pinochet in Chile, Syngman Rhee in South Korea, Lee Kuan Yew in Singapore, Chiang Kai-shek in Taiwan, or the present rulers of China were or are 'state dictators' in everything but name; but they presided or preside over an outstanding expansion and fast rising power of markets. All the countries named would not be today an epitome of the market's triumphs if it were not for the protracted 'dictatorship of the state'. Let's remember as well that the initial accumulation of capital invariably leads to an unprecedented and deeply resented polarization of life conditions and produces potentially explosive social tensions – which the up-and-coming entrepreneurs and merchants badly need to be suppressed and forcefully contained below the point of explosion by powerful and merciless, coercive state dictatorships.

Cooperation between state and market is a rule under capitalism; conflict between them, if it ever surfaces, is an exception. As a rule, the policies of the capitalist state, whether 'dictatorial' or 'democratic', are construed and conducted in the interests of, not against the interests of, the markets; their main (and intended, though not always overtly declared) effect is to endorse/enable/ensure the safety and longevity of the rule of the market. The second in the pair of 'recommodification' tasks discussed earlier, the task of the 'recommodification of labour', was no exception. However strong might be the moral considerations prompting the introduction of the 'welfare state', that state would hardly come about were it not for the factory owners who considered the care of the 'reserve army of labour' (keeping the reservists in good shape in case they were called back to active service) to be good – potentially profitable – investment. If the welfare state is now underfunded, falling apart or even actively dismantled, it is because the principal sources of capitalist profit have been relocated from the exploitation of factory labour to the exploitation of consumers. And because poor people, stripped of the resources needed to respond to the seductions of consumer markets, need currency, earned or borrowed (not a kind of service likely to be provided by the 'welfare state'), to be of any use in the current understanding of 'economic usefulness'.

CRM *After Prime Minister Gordon Brown went to the rescue of some institutions in the banking sector in Britain, following the first shock of the global financial crash of September 2008, Washington followed with a package of billions of dollars to rescue Wall Street, and subsequently, to rescue North American banks. Soon afterwards, other sectors rushed for the handout and kindly extended their begging hands for help.*

Like a piñata *at a children's party, where the big boys launch themselves into a huddle over the sweets and candy falling down from the heavenly toy, bankers and big corporations engulfed the crashed* piñata, *monopolizing all the goodies and leaving the shy, the timid and the youngest watching 'the big guys' grab what little there was to grab. It was the winter of 2008. Heads of state, environment ministers and senior government representatives who had converged in Poznan, Poland, at the United Nations Climate Change Conference were struggling to finalize a deal on climate change to cut greenhouse gases by a fifth by 2020.*[1] *At the very same time, in Washington, the biggest car industry corporations,*

General Motors, Chrysler and Ford, were demanding from the
Senate a $14 billion emergency bail-out. When this conversation
took place, it did not look as if the system was ready substantially
to invest in collective public transport and to gradually abandon
the car industry, nor was it ready to cut greenhouse gases radically
– the debate over biofuels (among other issues) continued between
those who believed that cereal ethanol is a greenhouse panacea,
and those who argue that biofuels require more carbon-emitting
fossil fuel than they displace, while also threatening water and
food security.[2]

In his time, when faced with recession in the last century, Presi-
dent Franklin D. Roosevelt ordered the car industry to stop pro-
ducing cars and produce tanks and aircraft instead (some would
say that this was, perhaps, because the war industry had the virtue
of 'killing two birds with one stone': the enemy and economic
recession). But in the young twenty-first century a new factor –
global warming – made things more complicated. The question
here being: can we really have another Franklin D. Roosevelt deal
in this century? If the car industry is not going to survive – whether
because there is no bail-out or because it becomes the igniting
factor in the last environmental catastrophe – what does the future
hold for the millions of families depending on the industry and
the millions of consumers worldwide depending on the economy
that the latter produces? And, finally, if no progress is made on
the climate change front, with the subsequent threats to water
supply and food scarcity and other environmental calamities –
water security allegedly being one of the greatest threats to peace
in the twenty-first century, as Luis Echeverria Álvarez, former
Mexican president and former director of the Centre for Economic
and Social Studies of the Third World, told me during a brief
interview)[3] *– are we at the threshold of another world war? Are*
we reaching the point where Rosa Luxemburg's snake is about to
devour and swallow its own head?

ZB   One event which the snake metaphor makes all but unthinkable is precisely the snake eating its own head. A snake's head
might be cryonized (cryonics, as Wikipedia informs us, is 'the
low-temperature preservation of humans and animals that can no
longer be sustained by contemporary medicine until resuscitation
may be possible in the future'), hoping that it can be revived at

some undefined moment when the rest of the body can be resur-
rected (there are quite a few state-constructed, lavishly state-
financed, though improvised, workshops where such hopes are
currently played with in the guise of prognoses and planning
targets); it might become food for scavengers (there are plenty of
them around, sniffing, slobbering, licking lips and sharpening
teeth), or part of the debris cluttering the site that needs to be
cleared for prospective buildings (the site-clearing equipment is
still with the designers and the designs of the future buildings are
still on their drawing boards) – or it might be just a warehouse of
slow-release nourishment for bacteria, and (when rediscovered by
the paleontologists of the coming centuries) a warehouse of topics
of endless debates, dissertations and clashes of opinion, and of
tools of academic promotion and celebrity one-upmanship. In all
these cases, the head would not disintegrate unless it was helped
into the nothingness from the outside . . .

What the snake metaphor (albeit obliquely) does imply, however,
is that the demise/collapse of capitalism is thinkable as an implosion rather than an explosion, let alone as destruction by an
external blow (if such a blow did come, it could only play the role
of a coup de grâce): capitalism will starve itself out of existence
once the pool of available/possible/imaginable grazing grounds is
exhausted. And according to the law of diminishing returns,
known all too well to any cultivator of land and any miner, the
effort to extract an extra morsel of useful/usable/profitable crop
turns exorbitantly costly as the pool nears the point of exhaustion
– rendering further cultivation or mining senseless and likely to
be abandoned before it becomes impossible.

We seem to have reached such a point; a point at which continuing along the road which brought us here is no longer on the
cards, however vehemently our guides may try to 'return to the
normal'. Just how traumatic the reaching of such a point may yet
prove to be beats our power to guess. You have rightly picked the
car industry as a sample of the 'normal' to which no return is
conceivable; if this is the case, however, how far and with what
devastating results will this particular tide reverberate? It has been
calculated that about a third of the US population derive their
living from servicing the car-dependent way of life. One recalls
what happened in the US when the extensive cultivation propelled
by the prospect of an easy dollar helped to reduce the fertile virgin

lands into a 'dust bowl', and hundreds of thousands of families
– like that of the *Grapes of Wrath* sharecropper Tom Joad –
having abandoned or been evicted from their homes and plots
of now barren land, took to the roads in search of land, jobs,
and dignity. And then, again rightly, you recall Franklin Delano
Roosevelt and ask: 'Can we really have another Franklin D.
Roosevelt deal in the twenty-first century?'

Well, it is not only generals who are inclined to plan and
fight the last successful war. Your question comes naturally –
Roosevelt's New Deal was no doubt a highly successful battle to
save capitalism against the most dire consequences of its inborn
suicidal tendencies. And so were the undertakings that in the
'developed' part of the postwar world emulated and developed the
Roosevelt idea of deploying the powers of state to insert some
logic and order into the endemically chaotic and illogical practices
of capitalism, guided as they are by one intention: the maximization of profits. We know now – we have been indeed oversupplied
with proof – that far from being a self-equilibrating system or
being moved by the 'invisible (but artful and astute) hand' of the
market, the capitalist economy produces massive instability which
it is blatantly unable to tame and control while using only its own,
so to speak, 'natural predispositions'. To put it bluntly, it generates
catastrophes which, by itself, it is unable to arrest, let alone to
prevent, just as it is unable to put right the damage that such
catastrophes perpetrate. The ability of 'self-correction' imputed to
the capitalist economy by some of its court economists boils down
to the periodical destruction of successful 'bubbles' (with outbursts of bankruptcies and mass unemployment) – and that at
enormous cost to the lives and prospects of those supposed to be
served by the benefits of capitalist endemic creativity . . .

In this respect, nothing has changed since Roosevelt's New
Deal. But the conditions under which that deal may be contemplated and put into operation have changed: a circumstance that
casts on any chance of its repetition the kind of doubt that Roosevelt and his counsellors did not have to reckon with. One thing
that has changed: the task Roosevelt faced was the 'Keynesian
challenge': to resuscitate, 'pump prime', lubricate and invigorate
industry, the principal employer and so obliquely the creator of
demand that would keep the market economy going and restart
the production of surplus needed for capitalist self-reproduction.

The present-day challenge reaches deeper, however: into the financial markets, not a massive employer but the indispensable and perhaps decisive link in the 'food chain' of all present and prospective employers. Any similarity between resuscitating an industry famished by the dearth of demand, and 'recapitalizing' financial institutions running short of funds to finance loans seems to be as misleading as it is superficial. As Hyman Minsky pointed out two decades ago, financial markets bear the main responsibility for capitalism's apparently incurable tendency to produce and reproduce its own instability and vulnerability; and as Paul Wooley has recently noted,[4] the ridiculously exorbitant size reached in recent years by purely financial and non-productive agencies is a function of the 'short-termism or momentum effect in stock markets', a tendency of stock markets that is impossible to stop and exceedingly difficult to mitigate. The latter has compared the unnaturally overgrown 'financial sector' to a tumour which, as is the habit of tumours, will eventually destroy the host organism if it is not excised in time. Therefore, if the state steps in, mobilizing the tax-paying potential of taxpayers and its own ability to borrow from abroad, in order to resuscitate financial agencies as Roosevelt resuscitated the American industries employing labour, it will only encourage the very 'short-termism and momentum effects' guilty of making the present catastrophe virtually unavoidable. Once lenders find out that there is a safety cushion in the form of the state rushing to help once the bluff of 'life on credit' is called and the lending–borrowing game has abruptly ended, then the sole thing that is likely to be 'resuscitated' is their willingness to speculate and take risks for the sake of immediate financial return, with little concern for the long-term consequences and sustainability of the game in the long run. The next bubble is bound to start growing. And let me add that what applies to the lenders applies as well, even if at an appropriately adjusted scale, to the borrowers with whom they are locked in a temptation–seduction loop. The object of credit transactions is not only the money lent and borrowed, but reinvigoration of 'short-termist' psychology and lifestyles. As it stretches to the point of bursting, the big bubble is surrounded by a multitude of personal or familial mini-bubbles bound to follow it to perdition.

Another thing that has radically changed since the time of the New Deal are the 'totalities' within which the economy may be reasonably expected to have its books balanced – if not to achieve self-sufficiency, then at least to approach the conditions of self-sustainability. Whatever may be presumed and suggested by the present resurrection of tribal sentiments and 'back to your tents, O Israel' policies (like Gordon Brown repeating after the British National Party the slogan 'British jobs for British people'), such a 'totality' can no longer be enclosed inside the borders of a single nation-state or even several confederated states. Such a 'totality' is now global. Governments may attempt to cut off their part of the globe from global trends and global terms of trade, but the effectiveness of the measures at their disposal is bound to be short-lived, and their longer-term effects risk being grossly counterproductive. The global 'space of flows', as Manuel Castells memorably named it, remains stubbornly beyond the reach of institutions confined to the 'space of places', including governments of states. All political boundaries are much too porous to ensure that the measures applied within the state's territory remain immune to the flows of capital that are bound to reverse the intended purpose of the exercise.

Karl Marx prophetically envisaged a situation in which capitalists, while moved exclusively by self-interest, would still welcome the state taking matters into its own hands and imposing on capitalist entrepreneurs the kinds of limitations they would not be able to initiate and accept individually as long as their competitors refused (and were free to refuse) to follow suit. Marx considered the cases of child labour or depressing wages below the poverty line: in the long run, such policies applied individually by capitalists in order to outsell the competition would necessarily stoke up trouble and spell disaster for them all, collectively, as the supplies of labour ran thin and the ability to work of people who were inadequately fed, shod, sheltered and trained fell and perhaps even dwindled to naught. Putting an end to such harmful and ultimately suicidal practices can only be accomplished collectively; it needs to be imposed – 'power-assisted', so to speak. In the name of salvaging the collective interests of capitalism, individual capitalists must be compelled by the powers that be, all of them together and at the same time, to compromise their own interests. More correctly, they must be forced to abandon the definition of self-interest imposed by unregulated, catch-as-and-what-you-can competition.

Roosevelt followed the pattern foreseen by Marx almost a hundred years earlier. So did other pioneers of the 'welfare state' in its many and diverse national forms. The postwar 'glorious thirty years' were the times when the combination of the memory of prewar depression and the experience of wartime mobilization of national resources (Roosevelt could command American car-makers to suspend all production of private cars and produce tanks and guns for the army instead) took the issue of communal (obligatory) insurance against the consequences of individual prof-iteering 'beyond left and right'.

But the 'glorious thirty years' were also the last time when all that action could be taken through legislation conceived, enacted and executed in the framework of a sovereign nation-state. Soon after that a new condition emerged, and too many book-balancing variables fell or were thrown out of the realm under the state's power of control (indeed, beyond the territory of the state's sovereignty) for insurance against the caprices and mischief of market-operated fate to be responsibly endorsed by single-country institutions. And as memories faded and experiences were forgot-ten, the 'social state' with its dense net of constraints and regula-tions lost its cross-class approval. Margaret Thatcher famously insisted that a pill won't cure unless it is bitter; what she failed to mention was that the bitter pills she administered (unchaining capital while chaining one by one all the forces potentially capable of taming its excesses) were to be swallowed by some to cure the discomforts of some others. What she did not mention either, in this case due to her ignorance aided and abetted by false prophets and myopic teachers, was that this sort of therapy must sooner or later cause an affliction which in various forms would affect every-body, and then bitter pills will have to be swallowed by everyone – or nearly everyone. This 'sooner or later' has presently turned into 'now'.

The pills which we, all of us, will have to swallow may grow still more bitter because the deafening noise of the 'credit crunch' has stifled or nearly stifled other alarms, no less urgent if not more so, making them less audible or altogether inaudible. Being seen to confront and tackle the noisiest alarms is a more effective elec-tion winner than responding to those others, and so it is more likely to attract the attention and earnest efforts of our elected leaders. Among the anticipations of the state of our common affairs in the next year, collected by the *Guardian* in its 27 December 2008 issue, we find Polly Toynbee's warning that according to the latest opinion polls only one in ten British citizens named climate change as a 'key national issue', the substantive majority pointing instead to crime and the economy. And the chances are, she adds, that 'the slump will shift climate change even further from public attention' – and further yet from governmental priorities. Madeleine Bunting hammers it home that nothing short of a 'value shift' will be needed to get us out of our present predicament; and that unlike in past bouts of depression, this time 'the value shift has to last for longer than a few years of recession'. 'But the almighty paradox', she adds, is that frugality (which we need in order to heal and sanitize our way of life and make our and our children's future a little bit more secure) 'is precisely what the politicians are urging us against, desperate to revive the economy' (an economy, let me add, taking the shape responsible for the present catastrophe; an economy which, as the politicians wish us to believe, has no valid alternative).

Conversation II

The welfare state in the age of economic globalization: the last remaining vestiges of Bentham's Panopticon. Policing or helping the poor?

Citlali Rovirosa-Madrazo *One of the most accepted arguments to explain the global financial collapse is that there was insufficient state regulation in our economy, particularly in the financial and banking sectors. It became widely accepted that, with the neoliberal policies imposed worldwide, since the administration of former president Ronald Reagan and, as you just mentioned, the premiership of Margaret Thatcher in the 1980s, the state 'shrank'; terms such as 'slim state', 'weak state', 'ghost state' and the like echoed all over the media in the aftermath of the financial downturn. Indeed, well before 2008, your own work pioneered political analysis in terms of 'the absent state' (as well as the 'absent society'), making recurrent references to this theme throughout, particularly in* Postmodernity and its Discontents *(1997) and, later on* Liquid Times *(2007).[1]*

Now, in contrast to the idea of poor regulation and the absent state, there is a paradox: if we consider the agencies of what some still call today the 'welfare state', they give the illusion of having an overwhelming, overpowering presence; they give the impression of containing solid, iron-like, overregulating bodies. Indeed, these agencies are highly regulatory; for those who find themselves relying on the institutions of social security in countries such as Britain and elsewhere in Europe, there seems to be little doubt about state 'intervention'. In fact, the welfare state seems to be carefully engineered as a solid mechanism to reproduce social and class hierarchy. And this complex engineering task involves, it seems, both macro and micro regulation. Unlike the type of regulation needed, according to some, to strengthen the state (in relation to the financial and banking sector), in the social security system everything is overregulated, to the last detail: no one is to be 'overpaid' in this meticulously organized structure. No generous or compassionate 'invisible hand' is in sight to help those in receipt of 'benefits' – no 'bail-out' for those depending on 'unemployment benefit' or other social security benefits: keep one fraction of one pound sterling more than 'what the law says you need to live on' (sic) and you will be prosecuted. This question, therefore, asks whether these are all just inconsistencies? Are they simply juxtapositions, are they paradoxes? Is the 'impossibility of the state' a testimony to its failure or a testimony to its success? Is over-regulation by the agencies of social security – in contrast with financial and banking under-regulation – a testament to the classist nature of the state and the role it plays in the reproduction of class hierarchy and inequality? Or are we simply recognizing a state that 'is', but perhaps 'does not exist' (now you see it, now you don't)?

Zygmunt Bauman The setting you describe is not the 'social state' – the name I suggested for the 'welfare state' in its initial intention and practice. In spite of the organizational/bureaucratic continuity between the social state and the setting you describe, and the apparent similarity of their clientele, they are, as the English say, 'very different kettles of fish'.

The social state, as originally advocated by Bismarck in Germany or Lloyd-George in Britain, was meant to promote the vital interests of the society of producers/soldiers, and to ensure its smooth functioning. The society of producers measured its strength by the numbers of able-bodied males fit to confront and endure the challenges of factory floor and battlefield. Even when they were not on active duty (unemployed factory workers, army reservists) they had to be kept ready to rejoin the ranks in case their labour or fighting force was needed: they had to be properly fed, clad, shod – they had to be in good health and live in decent conditions that allowed them to achieve and retain that health.

Whether paying the costs of all that was a good (indeed, necessary) investment of public funds was in a society of producers/
soldiers an issue 'beyond left and right', almost universally, even
if reluctantly, approved. The fight of the trade unions for state
insurance against the hardships of poverty and unemployment,
and the preaching and pressures of the morally sensitive part of
the public would be to no avail were it not for the overtly or tacitly
recognized role of the 'social state', consisting in what Jürgen
Habermas was to call, retrospectively, the 'recommodification of
capital and labour' (making capital able and willing to buy labour,
and labour attractive enough to buyers to be bought) – the crucial
activity of the state without which capitalism could not in the long
run survive.

As we move beyond the era of territorial conquests and mass
('Fordist') industry, the poor are no longer viewed as the reservists
for industry and the army, who must be kept in good shape since
they had to be ready at any moment to be called to active service.
Today, investment in the poor is not a 'rational investment'. The
poor are a perpetual liability rather than a potential asset. The
chances of their 'return to the ranks' of industry are slim, while
the new small and neat professional armies have no need of gun
fodder. The 'problem of the poor', once considered as social, has
been to a large extent redefined as a law and order issue. There is
a clear tendency to 'criminalize' poverty, as the substitution of the
term 'underclass' for the 'lower' or 'working' or 'destitute' classes
testifies (unlike those terms, 'underclass' intimates a category
'beneath', one that is outside, not the other classes, but the class
system, i.e. society, as such). The prime, defining purpose of the
state's concern with poverty is no longer keeping the poor in good
shape, but policing the poor, keeping them out of mischief and
out of trouble: controlled, surveilled, monitored, disciplined.
Agencies dealing with the poor and indolent are not a continuation of the 'social state'; in everything but name they are the last
remaining vestiges of Jeremy Bentham's Panopticon, or an updated
version of the poorhouses that preceded the advent of the welfare
state. They are much more the vehicles of exclusion rather than
inclusion; tools to keep the poor (i.e. the flawed consumers in a
society of consumers) out, not in.

Let's be clear about it: this is not evidence of the 'state's
schizophrenia', nor as you suggest of the 'impossibility of the

state'. The policies of the modern state, guided then and now by whatever is perceived to be in the 'interests of the economy', are now, as they were before, 'rational responses' – albeit adjusted to the changing state of society. The 'social state', at home in the society of producers, is an alien body and an awkward visitor in a society of consumers. There are few if any social forces that are in support of its idea, let alone mobilizing to force through its introduction and sustenance. For most of us in the society of consumers, the care for survival and welfare has been 'subsidiarized' by the state to individual concerns, resources and skills. What is wrongly named the 'welfare state' today is only a contraption to tackle the residue of individuals lacking the capacity to secure their own survival for lack of adequate resources. It is an agency to register, separate and exclude such people – and keep them excluded and securely isolated from the 'normal' part of society. That agency runs something like a ghetto without walls, a camp without barbed wire (though densely packed with watch towers!).

CRM *In* Postmodernity and its Discontents *and* Wasted Lives,[2] *as now, you discussed what you call the 'criminalization of poverty'. You sharply described how the welfare discourse was downgraded from a culture of citizens' rights to a culture of charity, humiliation and stigma.[3] You vividly describe the impact of the deregulation of the economy on our lives and of economic globalization; with your implacable pen you go on painfully to describe how 'the radical privatization of human fate goes along and apace with the radical deregulation of industry and finances'[4] and you consider the growing quantities of human beings living in deprivation. The question is now: is deregulation the only problem, or is it the fact that the rules of the game are constantly changing (regulation/deregulation in a pendulum movement) that fuels the flames? These agencies that you mentioned that run 'something like a ghetto without walls, a camp without barbed wire (though densely packed with watch towers!)', they also have, I think, the ability to play a role in the re-production and recycling of poverty and class hierarchy. Now I get the impression that, while you have defiant views on these institutions, you appear to have retained a degree of romantic hope in the original welfare state, which you insist we should regard as a 'social state' and* *prefer to see as a 'collective insurance policy'. Somehow I perceive a certain degree of ambivalence in the way you approach the original welfare state as it was inherited from postwar Britain. I am not sure if it is because of the way you treat it, almost as if 'you can't let go of it' (particularly in* The Absence of Society, *2008), or if it is because you want to suggest that it has not completed its transition to liquidity. Is this perhaps because, as I suggested above, we have solid, iron-like, overregulatory agencies of social security, which are, at the same time and notwithstanding, 'shrinking' and 'in danger of extinction' as increasingly more cuts are imposed? So where are we: mere paradoxes, inconsistencies, incomplete mutations?*

ZB Yes, you've put it splendidly: paradoxes, inconsistencies, incomplete mutations. In what we do (both in personal life and in history) we hardly ever start from a clean slate. The site on which we build is always cluttered: the past lingers in the same 'present' in which the future tries (sometimes by design, but mostly stealthily and surreptitiously) to take root. All continuity is stuffed with discontinuities; no discontinuity ('rupture', U-turn, 'new beginning') is free from residues and relics of the status quo ante. Adorno rightly warned that in trying to make our theoretical models consistent, harmonious, *eindeutig*, 'pure' and logically elegant (as we tend to do, and can't help doing, whenever we theorize), we inadvertently impute to reality more rationality than it possesses and could possibly acquire. All theoretical models are for that reason utopias (not necessarily in the sense of a 'good society', but certainly in that other sense of the word – of 'nowhere places'). Our theoretical models can breathe and move freely only in the habitat of academic offices, seminar rooms and scholarly symposiums – and rest only when ossified in their printed or video records. On the other hand, the messiness of our reports, offensive and offending as it is to a logic-loving mind, sometimes results from disorderly, sloppy thinking – but more often than not from a sober and faithful reproduction of the messiness of the reported objects.

But let's return to the object in the focus of our view: the 'welfare' (or 'social') state, and its present predicament. And let me point out at the start that the idea of the 'social state' was from the beginning pregnant with a contradiction that made it akin to the task of squaring a circle. That idea aimed at marrying freedom and security, the two values that are equally indispensable for a satisfying, or even just endurable, life, and yet are notorious for their 'love–hate' relation: each one unable to live without the other, yet neither able to live with the other (at least to live peacefully and cloudlessly). Freud famously defined civilization as the 'trade-off' between freedom and security. Security, he said, can be enhanced only at the expense of freedom, and whenever freedom grows, security diminishes. The idea of the social state was intended to break that rule. But can it be broken?

Our modern era started with the discovery of the 'absence of God'. The apparent randomness of fate (the lack of a visible connection between good fortune and virtue as much as between ill fate and vice) was taken as evidence that God abstains from active intervention in the world He created, having left human affairs to the worry of humans and their (Herculean, Superman-kind) efforts. The void thereby yawning at the world's control desk had to be filled by human society, attempting to replace blind fate with 'normative regulation', and existential insecurity with the rule of law; a society that would insure all its members against life risks and individually suffered misfortune. That intention found its fullest manifestation in the social arrangement commonly called the 'welfare state'.

More than anything else, the 'welfare state' (which, I repeat once more, I prefer to call by the name of the social state, a name that shifts the emphasis from the mere distribution of material benefits to the shared motive and purpose of their provision) was an arrangement of human togetherness invented as if precisely to prevent its present-day tendency, triggered, reinforced and exacerbated by the drive to 'privatize' (a shorthand for the promotion of the essentially anticommunal, individualizing patterns of the consumer market style – patterns that set individuals in competition with each other), the tendency to break down the networks of human bonds and undermine the social foundations of human solidarity. 'Privatization' shifts the task of fighting against and (hopefully) resolving socially produced problems onto the shoulders of individual men and women, in most cases much too weak for the purpose, depending on their mostly inadequate skills and insufficient resources – whereas the 'social state' tended to unite its members in an attempt to protect every and each of them from the morally devastating competitive 'war of all against all' and 'one-upmanship'.

A state is 'social' when it promotes the principle of communally endorsed, collective insurance against individual misfortune and its consequences. It is that principle – declared, set in operation and trusted to be in working order – that lifts the 'imagined society' to the level of a 'real' – tangibly sensed and lived – community, and thereby replaces (to deploy John Dunn's terms) the 'order of egoism', generating mistrust and suspicion, with the 'order of equality', inspiring confidence and solidarity. And it is the same principle which lifts members of society to the status of citizens: that is, makes them stakeholders, in addition to being stockholders – beneficiaries, but also actors responsible for the creation and decent allocation of benefits; citizens defined and moved by their acute interest in their common property in, and responsibility for, the network of public institutions that can be trusted to ensure the solidity and reliability of the state-issued 'collective insurance policy'.

Application of that principle may, and often does, protect men and women from the triple bane of poverty, impotence and humiliation; most importantly, however, it may (and by and large does) become a prolific source of social solidarity that recycles 'society' into a common, communal good. Society is raised to the level of community as long as it effectively protects its members against the twin horrors of misery and indignity, that is against the terrors of being excluded, of falling or being pushed over board from the fast accelerating vehicle of progress, of being condemned to 'social redundancy' and otherwise earmarked for 'human waste'.

In its original intention, the 'social state' was to be an arrangement to serve precisely such purposes. Lord Beveridge, to whom we owe the blueprint for the postwar British 'welfare state', was a liberal, not a socialist. He believed that his vision of a comprehensive, collectively endorsed insurance for everyone was the inevitable consequence and indispensable complement of the liberal idea of individual freedom, as well as a necessary condition of liberal democracy. Franklin Delano Roosevelt's declaration of war on fear was based on the same assumption, as must also have been Joseph Seebohm Rowntree's pioneering inquiry into the volume and causes of human poverty and degradation. Liberty of choice entails, after all, countless and uncountable risks of failure; many people would find such risks unbearable, fearing that they might exceed their personal ability to cope. For most people, the liberal ideal of freedom of choice will remain an elusive phantom and idle dream, unless the fear of defeat is mitigated by an insurance policy issued in the name of the community, a policy they can trust and rely on in the event of personal defeat or a blow of fate.

If freedom of choice is granted in theory but unattainable in practice, the pain of hopelessness will surely be topped with the humiliation of haplessness. Daily testing of the ability to cope with life's challenges is after all the very workshop in which the self-confidence of individuals, and so also their self-esteem, are cast – or melt away. Rescue from individual indolence or impotence cannot be expected from a political state that is not, and refuses to be, a social state. Without social rights for all, a large and in all probability a growing number of people will find their political rights being of little use and unworthy of their attention. If political rights are necessary to set social rights in place, social rights are indispensable to make political rights 'real' and keep them in operation. The two rights need each other for their survival; that survival can only be their joint achievement.

The social state has been the ultimate modern embodiment of the idea of community: that is, of an institutional reincarnation of such an idea in its modern form of an 'imagined totality' – woven of the awareness and acceptance of reciprocal dependence, of commitment, loyalty, solidarity and trust. Social rights are, so to speak, the tangible, 'empirically given' manifestations of that imagined totality, tying that abstract notion to daily realities and entrenching the imagination in the solid ground of daily life experience. These rights certify the veracity and realism of the mutual person-to-person trust, and of the individual's trust in the shared institutional network that endorses and validates collective solidarity. 'Belonging' translates as confidence in the benefits of human solidarity, and of the institutions that arise out of that solidarity and promise to serve it and assure its reliability. As was spelled out in the Swedish social democratic programme of 2004: 'Everyone is fragile at some point in time. We need each other. We live our lives in the here and now, together with others, caught up in the midst of change. We will all be richer if all of us are allowed to participate and nobody is left out. We will all be stronger if there is security for everybody and not only for a few.'

Just as the carrying power of a bridge is measured by the strength of its weakest pillar and grows together with that strength, the confidence and resourcefulness of a society is measured by the security and resourcefulness of its weakest section and grows as they grow. Social justice and economic efficiency, loyalty to the social state tradition and the ability to modernize swiftly and with little or no damage to social cohesion and solidarity are not and need not be at loggerheads. On the contrary, as the social democratic practice of our Nordic neighbours has demonstrated, 'the pursuit of a more socially cohesive society is the necessary precondition for modernization by consent.' That Scandinavian pattern is nowadays nothing but a relic of past hopes – of hopes once powerful, but now in large part frustrated.

Presently, however, we ('we' primarily belonging to the 'developed' countries, but – under the concerted pressure of global markets, the IMF and the World Bank – also belonging to most 'developing' ones) seem to be moving in an opposite direction: 'totalities' – societies and 'communities', real or even merely imagined – become increasingly 'absent'. The range of individual autonomy is expanding, but it also gets burdened with more and more functions that were once the responsibility of the state but have now been ceded ('subsidiarized') to individual self-concerns. States no longer endorse the collective insurance policy, leaving the task of achieving well-being and a secure future to individual pursuits.

Left increasingly to their own resources and acumen, individuals are expected to devise individual solutions to socially generated problems, and to do it individually, using their own individual skills and individually possessed assets. These expectations set individuals in mutual competition, and mean that communal solidarity (except in the form of temporary alliances of convenience: that is, of human bonds tied and untied on demand and with 'no strings attached'), is perceived as by and large irrelevant, if not downright counterproductive. Casting people into this position (unless it is mitigated by forceful institutional intervention) renders the differentiation and polarization of individual chances inescapable; indeed, it makes a self-propelling and self-accelerating process out of the polarization of prospects and chances. The effects of that tendency were easy to predict – and can now be counted. In Britain, for instance, the share of the top 1 per cent of earners has doubled since 1982 from 6.5 per cent to 13 per cent of national income, while chief executives of the FTSE 100 companies were earning (until the recent 'credit crunch' and beyond) not 20 times more than average earners, as in 1980, but 133 times.

This is not, however, the end of the story. Thanks to the new network of 'information highways', every individual – man or woman, adult or child, rich or poor – is invited (or compelled rather, given the notorious profligacy, ubiquity and obtrusiveness of the media) to compare their own individual lot with the lot of every other individual, and particularly with the lavish consumption of public idols (celebrities constantly in the limelight, on TV screens and the front pages of tabloids and glossy magazines) and to measure the values that make life worth living by the opulence they so ostentatiously brandish. At the same time, while the realistic prospects of a satisfying life continue to diverge sharply, the standards dreamed of and the coveted tokens of a 'happy life' tend to come into line (another 'inconsistency'!): the driving force of conduct is no longer the more or less realistic desire to 'keep up with Joneses', but the infuriatingly nebulous idea of 'keeping up with celebrities', catching up with supermodels, premier league footballers and top-ten singers. As Oliver James has recently suggested, a truly toxic mixture is created by stoking up 'unrealistic aspirations, and the expectations that they can be fulfilled'; but great swathes of the British population 'believe that they can become rich and famous', that 'anyone can be Alan Sugar or Bill Gates, never mind that the actual likelihood of this occurring has diminished since the 1970s'.[5]

So where does all that lead us? One lesson, I guess, becomes clearer by the day. Life in 'regulated' and 'deregulated' societies differs in very many respects – but the volume of happiness and the degree of immunity to unhappiness (already enjoyed, or likely to be provided and obtained) are not among them. Each of the two kinds of society has its own kinds of suffering, agony and fears.

We know now that deregulation, promoted under the slogan of more freedom, of the emancipation of human daring and human initiative from the petty constraints cramping their movements and liberty of choice, resulted, in the end, in a chorus of its promoters of yesterday singing the praises of state intervention and of enforced, power-assisted salvage from the catastrophe triggered by deregulated freedoms. 'Deregulation' is fast turning into a dirty word, whereas the dirty words of yesterday – such as public expenditure, state enterprise and compulsory regulation, even nationalization – are being hastily cleaned of all the grime that stuck to them in the three decades of 'emancipation'. For the moment no one can say how protracted that astonishing turn will prove to be – but currently the pendulum is swinging in an opposite direction to the 'deregulating' logic. As we've learned from school physics, however, in the course of each swing the 'kinetic' energy that keeps the pendulum moving tends to diminish, while the 'potential' energy (the energy that will turn 'kinetic' the moment the pendulum changes its direction again) gathers volume. That rule seems to apply to all pendulums – including the one that swings to and fro between regulation and deregulation, or security and freedom . . .

Conversation III

This thing called 'the state': revisiting democracy, sovereignty and human rights

Citlali Rovirosa-Madrazo *In the last decades, the 'epistemological break' with modernity and the spread of so-called postmodern and poststructuralist thinking have resulted in challenging and seductive ideas. Few have eluded their enchanting, alluring charm. I myself did not escape the bewitching love affair. This may be why, in 1995, I ventured to write that the nation-state (and indeed the state), as well as other peculiar institutions of our civilizations, were only ethnocentric constructions, indeed Western patriarchal illusions (not that I have retracted . . .).[1] Since our irresistible love affair with post-modernism, we have all rebelled against our European and Mediterranean 'parents' (from the Judeo-Christian tradition to the Greeks, and then Marx, and beyond; from modernity to postmodernity and back); we have all drunk from the postmodern grail (wasn't it refreshing? indigestible, I'd say). But what is now going to save us from what often seems to be the 'collapse' of 'pretty much everything'? What are the prospects of utopia, and how have you felt about it since (. . . do you remember when you wrote 'Socialism descended upon nineteenth-century Europe as utopia'?).[2] In other words, where do we go from here? (Sorry for the burden placed upon you . . .)*

Zygmunt Bauman The 'real collapse of pretty much everything', the likely ultimate destination of a tendency dominant in our present form of life, is not 'here' – at any rate not yet. But until quite recently it seemed that it might be; or at least that it was about to arrive, and soon . . .

In Michel Houellebecq's *The Possibility of an Island*,[3] the final sentences jotted down by Daniel25, the last (by his own choice) in a long (infinite by design) series of cloned Daniels, are:

> I had perhaps sixty years left to live; more that twenty thousand days that would be identical. I would avoid thought in the same way I would avoid suffering. The pitfalls of life were far behind me; I have now entered a peaceful space from which only the lethal process would separate me . . .
>
> I bathed for a long time under the sun and the starlight, and I felt nothing other than a lightly obscure and nutritive sensation . . .
>
> . . . I was, I was no longer. Life was real.

Somewhere in between these meditations, Daniel25 concludes: 'Happiness was not a possible horizon. The world had betrayed him.' In Houellebecq's rendering, this was to be the end. But what was the beginning? How had it all started?

Twenty-five clonings earlier, in the heady, intoxicating times of what you call the 'epistemological transgression', and before the 'First' and the 'Second Decrease' of the human population of the planet (code names for credit collapse? or ecological collapse?) – catastrophes destined to transform whatever remained of the erstwhile human species into scattered gangs of cannibalistic savages, and to leave the memory of the human past to the sole possession, guardianship and care of 'neohumans': the endlessly self-cloning, 'equipped with a reliable system of reproduction and an autonomous communication network' and 'gathered in enclaves protected by a fail-safe security system' in order to 'shelter from destruction and pillage the whole sum of human knowledge' (a motive which Daniel25 would retrospectively impute) – Daniel1 (the last of the Daniels born to a mother) noted in his diary: 'I no longer feel any hate in me, nothing to cling to any more, no more landmarks or clues . . . There is no longer any real world, no world, no human world, I am outside time, I no longer have any past or future, I have no more sadness, plans, nostalgia, loss or hope . . .'

As Daniel25 would also note twenty-five neohuman clones later, in a stark contradiction of his hypothesis as to the original

motives of the whole affair, Daniel1 was 'particularly eloquent'
on that theme – of nostalgia for desire. That nostalgia, as we are
allowed to guess, was what more than anything else prompted
him to embrace the offer of the ultimate New Beginning: of an
endless string of resurrections/reincarnations/new births in the
form of cloned replicas of preceding selves. No wonder the first,
still born-of-a-mother member in the series of cloned Daniels
found the offer alluring, since 'in real life', as he noted (read: in
the life he knew, the only life he could have known before infinite
cloning became a realistic prospect), the chances of 'new begin-
nings' grind to a halt (sooner rather than later!): 'Life begins at
fifty, that's true; insomuch as it ends at forty' . . .

By all standards of happiness, the first Daniel was the epitome
of success: he was a darling of the chattering classes, awash with
money, always in the limelight, with a supply of female charms
outstripping his ability to consume them. One fly in that sweet
ointment he bewailed, however, and bitterly, was the infuriating
finality of it all. You might have played down or ignored the
spectre of the end . . . till you were forty. Not much longer than
that, though! But the 'happiness bit' needs to be cleansed of the
worry about an end – just as the exhilaration brought about by
the state of intoxication must be uncontaminated by the prospect
of an imminent hangover. In the times of Daniel1 – our real time,
yours and mine – the pursuit of happiness rests on the assumption
of endless self-repetition: in this respect, at least, our concept of
'living for the sake of happiness and ever greater happiness' is
perhaps the archetype of the project of cloning, immortality's
high-tech, state of-the-art substitute.

But the prospect of an unavoidable end worms its way towards
you stealthily, without you noticing, and once you are between
forty and fifty years of age it settles here, in the place you call 'the
present', catching you as a rule unprepared and baffled. After all,
little if anything in your successful life taught you and drilled into
your life the end's obtrusive while ineluctable company. Suddenly,
what you've been trained for and came to consider 'life', that
luxuriant stream of pleasures, runs thin and comes ever closer to
drying up. Daniel then recalls and grasps the sinister message in
Schopenhauer's warning: 'No one can see above himself.' Fortunately for him, Isabelle, the elusive object of his desire, was still
around (shortly before she disappeared from his life forever), and
'at that moment Isabelle could see above me'.

And what did Isabelle see? In her own words, she saw that 'when you grow old you need to think of reassuring and gentle things. You need to imagine that something beautiful awaits us in heaven.' And then she mused: we train ourselves for death – when we aren't too stupid; or too rich. Being too rich (or too stupid – but if you were stupid, then, according to the definition of stupidity, you wouldn't know anyway) you'd find it terribly difficult to imagine an end to serial pleasures; if you ever tried to imagine it, that is. Seeing comes, in this case, before the imagination takes off. The end must first stare you in the face before you find out how inconceivable (more to the point, unendurable) it is.

It took Daniel twenty-five successive rebirths to note: 'The joys of humans remain unknowable to us (neohumans); inversely, we cannot be torn apart by their sorrows. Our nights are no longer shaken by terror or by ecstasy. We live, however; we go through life, without joy and without mystery.'

It was that discovery, we are allowed to guess, that prompted Daniel25 to revoke Daniel1's decision and to choose what Daniel1 wished to escape: to surrender (reject, rather) his perpetuity/infinity of existence assured by cloning, and cut himself free from the future (that is, of future rebirths of the same). 'I was, like all neohumans, immune to boredom . . . I was . . . a long way from joy, and even from real peace: the sole fact of existing is already a misfortune. Departing from, at my own free will, the cycle of rebirth and deaths, I was making my way towards a simple nothingness, a pure absence of content.' Daniel25 himself pronounced that sentence (as there was no one around who, there and then or in the future, could do it for him): the sentence of 20 thousand days in purgatory separating him from the paradise of non-existence, a vision he could describe best in words borrowed from Samuel Beckett:

> there is only me, this evening, here, on earth, and a voice that makes no sound because it goes towards none . . . See what is happening here, where there's no one, where nothing happens . . . I know, there is no one here, neither me nor anyone else, but some things are better left unsaid, so I say nothing. Elsewhere perhaps, by all means, elsewhere . . . [But] what elsewhere can there be to this infinite here?[4]

Indeed, having imbibed all that was available to be devoured, and with nothing in the past, present or future safe from its omnivorous voracity, infinity equals the impossibility of an 'elsewhere'. And what the neohumans managed, tragically, to forget was that without some 'elsewhere' beyond a specific number of next corners or next mornings, there is not, and can't be, humanity. At least the kind of humanity as we all, including the writers of dystopias, know it.

In a remarkable article on the persistence of utopia,[5] Miguel Abensour quotes William Morris insisting in 1886 that 'men fight and lose the battle, and the thing that they fought for comes about in spite of their defeat, and when it comes it turns out not to be what they meant, and other men have to fight for what they meant under another name . . .[6] Morris was writing about all men, 'men as such', assuming and suggesting that fighting for a 'thing that is not' is the way humans, all humans, are: is, indeed, the defining trait of 'being human'. He believed that for men (and we would add: or women) fighting for such a thing is a must, such a fight being in their nature ('The "Not" [or Nicht]', as Ernst Bloch pointed out, 'is lack of Something and also escape from that lack; thus it is driving toward what is missing'[7]). If we agree with Morris, we can take utopias to be elaborate, systematized expressions of that crucial aspect of human nature. Utopias were so many attempts to spell out in detail and describe in full that 'thing' for which the next fight was to be launched.

Let us note though, right away, that however much they might have varied in all other respects, all utopias written by Morris's predecessors and contemporaries (including by Morris himself), a hundred or more years before the vision of serial Daniels could possibly germinate in Houellebecq's visionary mind, were blueprints of a world in which battles for 'things that are not' would no longer be on the cards: those battles would be neither required nor wished for, as the last stone would already have been turned, and turning over any more stones could only detract from the perfection already reached. So, if we agree with Morris, the 'big thing' missed and thus fought for by people who had it in their nature to fight for things missing and missed (whatever name they gave to the thing they currently fought for – a temporary and on the whole contentious name) was, paradoxically, the end to fighting; the end to a need or a drive, and a desire to fight, and to its desirability. And the big thing that kept 'coming about' in the aftermath of lost battles (that only turned out 'not to be what they were meant to be' and to prompt other people to fight again for the same thing under a different name) was the condition of having no fight on one's hands; just like the armistice that follows the hostilities, and as a rule is found to fall well short of the bliss that it was imagined and hoped that the peace fought for would be. The restlessness of the compulsive and addicted draughtsmen and chasers after utopias was propelled and sustained by the intractable desire for a rest. People ran into battle chasing the dream of laying down arms – forever.

Another defining feature of utopias in William Morris's times (and for almost a century afterwards) was their radicalism. Acts, undertakings, means and measures may be called 'radical' when they reach down to the roots: of a problem, a challenge, a task. Note, however, that the Latin noun '*radix*', to which the meta-phorical uses of 'radical' trace their pedigree, refers not only to roots, but also to foundations and to origins. What do these three notions – root, foundation and origin – have in common? Two attributes.

One: under normal circumstances, the material referents of all three can be only surmised, guessed, imagined – they are, after all, hidden from view and impossible to examine, let alone be sensu-ally experienced. All that has grown out of them (their 'outgrowth' – such as trunks or stems in the case of roots, edifices in the case of the foundations, or consequences in the case of the origins) has wrapped them in a tightly knit, dense and impermeable tissue of 'later history', having emerged into view by covering them up and hiding them from view in its shadow; and so, if one wishes to reach the target of thinking or acting 'radically', that tissue has first to be pierced, hurled out of the way or taken apart.

Two: in the course of blazing a trail towards that target, the outgrowth needs to be notionally deconstructed, or materially 'pushed out of the way' or dismantled. The probability is high that the target will emerge from the work of deconstruction and dismantling disabled once and for all – for all practical purposes incapacitated. It might no longer be able to give birth to, offer a site for, or start off another growth, particularly an outgrowth replicating the one that has been decomposed or stifled. Taking a 'radical' stance signals an intention to destroy – or, at any rate, a readiness to take the risk of destruction; more often than not, a radical stance aims at a 'creative destruction' – destruction in the sense of 'site clearing', or turning over and loosening the soil, in order to prepare for another round of sowing or planting and make the ground ready to accommodate another type of root. One takes a 'radical stance' when accepting all those conditions, and guiding oneself by all such intentions and objectives.

Russell Jacoby distinguishes two sometimes coinciding, yet not necessarily interconnected, traditions in modern utopian thought: the 'blueprint' ('The blueprint utopians map out the future in inches and minutes') and the 'iconoclastic' (iconoclastic utopians 'dreamt of a superior society' but 'declined to give it precise measures').[8] I propose to retain the name Jacoby suggests for the second, admittedly 'non-blueprint', utopian tradition, but to modify its meaning slightly: to focus the concept on attributes other than the vagueness or deliberate imprecision. The meaning I suggest is intimated by the very idea of 'iconoclasm', and refers to the intention to deconstruct, demystify and ultimately to debunk the dominant life values and strategies of the time. 'Iconoclastic' utopias are those that show that the pursuit of those values and strategies, instead of ensuring the advent of a superior society or superior life, constitutes an insurmountable obstacle on the road to either. In other words, I propose to unpack the concept of 'iconoclastic utopia' as a focusing (as in all utopias) on a critical revision of the ways and means of the present life as the main factor in an uncovering of the otherwise suppressed and concealed, and hitherto unknown, possibility of an 'else-where', of another 'social reality'. This being the prime interest and preoccupation of 'iconoclastic utopias', it is no wonder that the alternative to the present remains sketchy; a vagueness of the anticipatory vision is simply a derivative of the prime concern. The principal stake of iconoclastic utopianism is the possibility of an alternative social reality, not its precise design. Iconoclastic utopias presume, whether overtly or tacitly, that the road to a 'superior society' leads not by way of the drawing boards of draughtsmen, those advanced troops or quartermasters of the future, but through critical reflection on the extant human practices and beliefs, unmasking (to recall Bloch's idea) that 'Something that is missing' and so inspiring the drive to its creation or recovery.

In William Morris's time, utopias tended to be on the 'blueprint' side. I believe that the time of iconoclastic utopias has arrived instead (though I wouldn't bet on how long they will stay) – in a package deal with liquid modernity, obsessive/compulsive DIP (deregulation, individualization, privatization) and consumerism. The better those utopias settle, the clearer becomes the eventual/ anticipated/imminent destination of life under their aegis. Each kind of utopia is pregnant with its own dystopias – genetically determined, as all offspring are. When they move into the Lebenswelt, the embryos turn into inner demons . . .

CRM   *In your work, particularly 'The rise and fall of labour',*[9] *you examined the history and development of the Labour Party. Indeed, Labour turned out to be something very different from what it set out to be in its early days and, in fact, when it took power in 1997. What went wrong? Was it as simple a matter as the party betraying its principles, or was it more complex than that: was it a case of the Western paradigm of party politics and democracy, themselves, having been condemned to fail anyway? In other words, where does the failure (or betrayal) of the left leave the Western habit of (addiction to) democracy? I suppose that what I am trying to ask is: is democracy also an illusion (a Western myth), another wobbly institution?*

Has democracy, perhaps, been stubbornly constructed as an ultimate destination of humanity – the ecumenical and teleological destiny of the 'civilized world'? If so, what hope is there for us? (We learnt from the last decade of the twentieth century that, on the other side of Atlantic, several indigenous organizations across Latin America, particularly the Zapatistas in South-East Mexico, shook democracy off their agenda when they engaged, as early as 1994, in what I called the first postmodern revolution of the twentieth century.[10] *A handful of indigenous women and men of Mayan ancestry had challenged the Western tradition of democracy, setting out to develop new forms – or rather setting out to reinvent very ancient traditions indeed of conducting politics.*[11] *In their view, 'direct democracy' rather than re-present-ative democracy (no longing for the 'metaphysics of presence' in their approach) was the only hope for building a better world. Thus the vacancy left by what Zapatistas perceived as 'incompetent, racist and corrupted' political parties across the spectrum in Mexico was filled*

*with the Juntas del Buen Gobierno or Councils of Good Govern-
ment which, according to the Spanish philosopher Luis Villoro,[12]
show that 'another vision of the world is possible' (in his view,
'such another world is already here, not as a Utopia, but as a
"real", "existing" place'). What, in short, in your opinion is the
relevance of the paradigm of democracy in today's transitions? Is
it time to unveil the myths behind the concept?*

ZB About half a century ago T. H. Marshall recycled the
popular mood of his time into a (ostensibly, as it later transpired)
universal law of human progress: from property rights to political
rights, and from them to social rights. About a quarter of a
century later Kenneth Galbraith spotted another regularity, bound
to seriously modify/correct, if not downright refute Marshall's
prognosis: as the universalization of social rights begins to bring
fruit, more and more bearers of political rights tend to use their
voting entitlements to support individual initiative, with all its
consequences – growing, rather than diminishing, inequality of
incomes, standards of living, and life prospects. Galbraith ascribed
this trend to the sharply different mood and life philosophy of
the emergent 'contented majority', who – feeling firm in the
saddle and at home in the world of great risks but also of great
opportunities – saw no need of the 'welfare state'. The 'welfare
state' was an arrangement they experienced ever more strongly
and harrowingly as a cage rather than a safety net, a constraint
rather than an opportunity; and also as a wasteful largesse which
they, the majority of the contented, able to rely on their own
resources, would in all probability never need and from which
they would in no imaginable way benefit. The widespread,
'beyond left and right' support for the social state, seen by T. H.
Marshall as the ultimate destination of the 'historical logic of
human rights', started to shrink, crumble and vanish with accelerating speed.

Another quarter of a century has passed, and socio-political
realities seem to match Galbraith's, instead of Marshall's,
prognosis.

Gerhard Schröder is on record as declaring, ten years ago, in
the heady times of the honeymoon of the 'Third Way' and 'New
Labour', that 'economic policy' 'is neither left nor right. It is either
good or bad.' Ten years later, we are able to conclude that this

assumption, once it was embraced, acquired all the powers of a
self-fulfilling prophecy – though the form of its fulfilment did not
match the intentions that prompted the prophets to prophesize
. . . When their prophecy/declaration was made public, eleven out
of fifteen governments of the European Union as it was then were
run by socialists. Now, in election after election, country after
country, the left is elbowed out of positions of power. In the ten
years preceding the reversal of the trends, social, democratic
parties presided over the 'economic policy' of the privatization of
gains and the nationalization of losses. They ran states preoccu-
pied with deregulation, privatization and individualization. At
the end of that decade, Gordon Brown leads the all-European
effort to mobilize 'taxpayers' into the campaign to recapitalize
the capitalist economy, thereby temporarily salvaging it from the
consequences of its own greed and in-built suicidal tendency, and
bringing banking, moneylending and an economy run on credit
'back to normal'. There is nothing, or almost nothing, left to
distinguish the 'left' from the 'right' in economic, or any other
policy; though, by common, left/right consent, those policies that
are neither right nor left are anything but 'good'.

Today, there is no distinctly 'left' vision or credible programme
that would appeal to the imagination of electors and convince
them that 'good economic policy' may be synonymous with the
'left economic policy'. Following the line of Third Way thinking,
to be 'left' means to be able to do more thoroughly the job that
the 'right' demands to be done but fails to do properly. It was
Tony Blair's 'New Labour' that laid the institutional foundations
under Margaret Thatcher's inchoate ideas of 'there is no society,
only individuals and families', of her rampant individualization,
privatization and deregulation. It was the French Socialist Party
that did most for the dismantling of the French social state. And
as to the 'postcommunist' parties in East-Central Europe, renamed
as 'social democrats' – wary as they are of being accused of their
still unextinguished devotion to their communist past – they are
the most enthusiastic and vociferous advocates and most consistent practitioners of unlimited freedom for the rich and of leaving
the poor to their own care.

Over more than a century the distinctive mark of the left was
to believe that it is the sacrosanct duty of community to care for
and to assist all its members, collectively, against the powerful

forces they are unable to fight alone. Social democratic hopes of performing that task used, however, to be invested in the sovereign modern nation-state, powerful and ambitious enough to limit the damage perpetuated by the free play of the markets by forcing economic interests to respect the political will of the nation and the ethical principles of national community. But nation-states are no longer as powerful as they used to be or hoped to become. The political states that once claimed full military, economic and cultural sovereignty over their territory and its population are no longer sovereign in any of those aspects of common life. The condition sine qua non of effective political control over economic forces is that political and economic institutions should operate at the same level – this is not, however, the case today. Genuine powers, the powers that decide the range of life options and life chances of most our contemporaries, have evaporated from the nation-state into the global space, where they float free from political control: politics has remained as local as before and therefore is no longer able to reach them, let alone constrain them. One of the effects of globalization is the divorce between power (in the sense of the German *Macht* – the capacity to have things done) and politics. We have now power emancipated from politics in the global space (the 'space of flows', in Manuel Castells's language), and politics deprived of power in the local space ('space of places' in the vocabulary of the same author).

That development has left socialists without the crucial (the only?) instrument intended to be used in the implementation of their project. Simply, a 'social state' guaranteeing existential security to all can no longer be constructed, or survive, in the framework of the nation-state (the forces that would have to be tamed for that purpose are not under the nation-state's command). Attempts to use the weakened state for that purpose have been foiled in most cases under the pressure of extraterritorial, global economic forces or markets. Increasingly, social democrats have revealed their sudden inability to deliver on their promise. Hence the desperate effort to find another trademark and legitimation; the Italian Democratic Party, or for that matter the Polish 'Left and Democrats', exemplify the destination to which that search leads: a total absence of trademark and legitimation. In that ultimate form, the distant offspring of the left of the past can count only on the failures of their adversaries as their sole electoral chance, and on the disaffected and angry victims of those failures as their only electoral constituency.

The first collateral casualty was the issue of 'existential security'. That past jewel in the left's crown has been dropped by the parties wrongly called 'left'; it lay, so to speak, on the street – from which it was promptly picked up by forces equally wrongly called 'right'. The radically right-wing Italian Lega is now promising to restore existential security – which the Democratic Party, claiming to be the legitimate heir of the Italian left and its chief spokesperson, promises to further undermine by more deregulation of capital and trade markets and more flexibility in the labour market, and by opening the country's doors yet wider to mysterious, unpredictable and uncontrollable global forces (doors which – as it knows from its own bitter experience – cannot be locked at any rate). Only, fraudulently, the new populist right interprets the causes of existential insecurity differently from the left of the past: not as a product of a capitalist free-for-all (freedom for the high and mighty, impotence for the lowly and resourceless), but (in the case of Italy) as the outcome of well-off Lombardians being forced by Rome to share their wealth with indolent Calabrians or Sicilians, and of the imposition of a need, common to them all, to share their means of living with foreigners (forgetting that the immigration of millions of ancestors of twenty-first century Italians to the US and Latin America enormously contributed to their present riches).

But you've asked a yet more fundamental question which as far as I am concerned is still waiting for a convincing answer: what is the relevance of the 'democratic paradigm' in the current climate? To sharpen that question still further: to what extent can hopes of a 'good society' (whatever contents one might put into this phrase) be invested in the democratic form of human cohabitation and self-government? Churchill famously said that democracy is the worst political system except for all the others – but just how satisfactory is that 'least evil of the evil forms of political rule'? And to what extent we can rely on it to resolve the problems arising from our togetherness?

Henry Giroux recently observed that

> democracy is not simply about people wanting to improve their lives; it is more importantly about their willingness to struggle to

protect their right to self-determination and self-government in the interest of the common good. Under the reign of free market fundamentalism, market relations both expanded their control over public space and increasingly defined people as either consuming subjects or commodities, effectively limiting their opportunity to learn how to develop their full range of intellectual and emotional capacities to be critical citizens.[13]

He also quoted Sheldon Wolin to the effect that if 'democracy is about participating in self-government, its first requirement is a supportive culture of complex beliefs, values, and practices to nurture equality, cooperation, and freedom.'[14] And I wonder whether those 'beliefs and practices' of 'equality, cooperation, and freedom' can be produced and entrenched by the logic of the 'really existing' democracy of the day, as it can be deduced from the activities of our governments (it seems that the Zapatistas had good reasons to doubt whether that is, or could be, the case). Is the spirit of equality, cooperation and freedom a product of democracy, or its preliminary condition – a factor unlikely to emerge from governmental practice if it was not already in place? As I feel and you probably see, it is not just that convincing answers to those fundamental questions are thus far absent, but that the questions themselves are not yet sufficiently articulated to prepare the ground for answers.

I suspect that our doubts about the ability of our kind of institutions of democracy to promote 'equality, cooperation and freedom', as well as our dark premonitions about its future chances of self-critique and self-reform, derive, so to speak, not so much from the ways democratic institutions are structured and operate but from the nature of the society those institutions are presumed/hoped/obliged to serve. Modern democracy was born out of the needs and ambitions of a society of producers; the ideas of 'self-determination' and 'self-government' were made to the measure of producers' skills and practices of production. The big question, to my mind, is whether such ideas can survive the passage from a society of producers to one of consumers? From a society seen as a collective product of shared labour to a society perceived as a container of goods for grabs – for appropriation, enjoyment and prompt disposal – as it tends to be viewed when it is looked at from the perspective of consumerists' preoccupations and life strategies. In other words, are democratic institutions endemically inclined to promote collective values over individualistic values, the cooperative over the competitive, an 'order of equality' over an 'order of egoism'? Or are democratic structures of governance similar to vending machines, only giving out what was put inside them in the first place?

One way or the other, much has been done in recent decades by democratically elected governments to recast the citizen into a consumer of state-offered services, and the ideal citizen as a satisfied, uncomplaining client. To all practical intents and purposes, democratically elected governments acquitted themselves rather impressively in the task of agent of the commodity market and seller of its worldview, values and practices.

Jerry Z. Muller, professor of history at the Catholic University of America, has stated recently that 'ethnonationalism', an ideology identifying the sense of belonging, loyalty and commitment as focused on the genuine or putative sharing of origin (French school textbooks starting with 'Our ancestors, the Gauls', or Churchill addressing 'this island race'), is on the rise around the globe.[15] In parts of the planet where the conflict-ridden modern process of matching nationhood to statehood is just beginning or still incomplete, that rise of ethnonationalistic sentiments is hardly surprising. But Muller's generalization encompasses the 'old democracies', countries where it is almost universally considered that the ethnonationalistic fury of the nation-building era has long since been replaced, once and for all, with cool, peaceful and benevolent 'liberal nationalism' (or, to deploy Jürgen Habermas's phrase, 'constitutional patriotism) – and this is a puzzling, and by all accounts surprising, development. 'Ethnonationalism', Muller explains, 'draws much of the emotive power from the notion that the members of a nation are part of an extended family'. Here, I suggest, lies the secret. 'Family' brings to mind an unending mutual commitment, an equality of entitlements, a secure (because irrevocable) recognition of rights, and particularly of the right to share in good fortune and the readiness of all to share in fortune's unlucky turns. 'Community' stands for such an 'extended family' in our world map – and the social state was a protracted and tortuous attempt to raise the togetherness of the state's citizens to the rank of a 'national community'. Today, however, every and any state, to one degree or another, tussles with a sort of 'double

bind', or divided and often antagonistic, if functionally intertwined, loyalties. Governments need to match the expectations of
their community-seeking voters while simultaneously abiding by
the demands of global forces intrinsically hostile to all and any
community-style enclosure and autarkic ambition. The two pressures are all too often jarringly at odds; one of their effects is the
waning of the nation's trust in being properly represented by their
democratically elected representatives, and so, by proxy, in democracy. Certainly, in opting out of the government-administered
public arena and seeking a more secure and more community-like
shelter in 'direct democracy' the Zapatistas made a predictable
effort to reanchor the trust that had been set loose and made
homeless, and selected for that purpose one of the two conceivable
responses to what they perceive as a betrayal of interests by state
powers. The other response, ever more widely tried by democratically elected governments when they resort to populists' vocabulary – hopes against hope to resurrect the marriage between state
and nation, now on the brink of divorce. While trying to strengthen
their hand in their effort to capitalize on the xenophobic and
parochial impulses of the orphaned national community, state
governments willy-nilly leave their other flank exposed and vulnerable to swift and hard-hitting retaliation by global capital – the
consequences of which, contrary to the usage of xenophobic
vocabulary, are very unlikely to endear them in the eyes and hearts
of the electorate they wish to entice. And yet this is a quandary
from which there is little prospect of promptly finding an escape
– at a time when, for instance, as Edmund L. Andrews reported
in the *New York Times* of 7 February, 2008:

> The Labor Department [of the US government] said that almost
> 600,000 jobs disappeared in January and that a total of 3.6 million
> jobs had been lost since the beginning of the recession in December
> 2007. The unemployment rate, meanwhile, rose to 7.6 percent,
> from 7.2 percent a month earlier. Losing more than a half million
> jobs in each of the last three months, the country is trapped in a
> vortex of plunging consumer demand, rising joblessness and a
> deepening crisis in the banking system.

And when similar reports are fast becoming daily bread for the
citizens of all or almost all the old democracies.

In a sense, democracy's upper hand over tribal sentiments and sectarian divisions was, not unlike the 'sub-prime mortgage affair', due in large measure to the expectation of the value of assets obtained rising forever faster than the volume of accruing liabilities. And again not unlike in the sub-prime mortgage case, that expectation has been proved unwarranted – with social and political consequences difficult to prognosticate at this early stage.

CRM *Let me now briefly bring back the question of the state in this context. In a report compiled and published by the United Nations and the European Union, O'Donnell* et al. *developed compelling arguments about the symbiotic nature of the relationship between state and democracy.*[16] *Broadly speaking, the report seemed to be suggesting that, without a solid state, there is no democracy. In the analysis (focused mostly on Latin American societies), it is concluded that, in order to preserve democracy, the state must be consolidated. I cannot help asking, is this the right order in the equation? Does one really set out to 'rescue the state' for the sake of democracy?*

ZB The state – whether in its present-day married-to-nation and territorially confined form, or in any other form as yet untested, unknown or even at the moment inconceivable, is indispensable not 'for the sake of democracy' (saying that would be like putting the cart before the horse), but for the sake of making the equality of humans feasible (I would even say 'dreamable'), if not real.

Class is just one historical form of inequality, the nation-state one of its historical frames, and 'the end of national class society' (if indeed the era of the 'national class society' has ended, which is a moot question) does not augur 'the end of social inequality'. We now need to extend the issue of inequality beyond the misleadingly narrow area into which it is commonly squeezed, focused narrowly on GNP or 'income per head', to the fatal mutual attraction between poverty and social vulnerability, corruption and the accumulation of dangers, as well as humiliation and the denial of dignity – the group-integrating (more correctly, in their case, disintegrating) factors shaping attitudes and conduct, fast growing in importance in an age of the globalization of information.

I believe that what lies beneath the present 'globalization of inequality' is the current repetition, though this time on a planetary scale, of the process spotted by Max Weber in the origins of modern capitalism and dubbed by him the 'separation of business from household': in other words, the emancipation of business interests from all extant socio-cultural institutions of ethically inspired supervision and control (concentrated at that time in the family household/workshop and through it in the local community) – and consequently the immunization of business pursuits against all values other than the maximization of profit. With the benefit of hindsight, we can view the present departures as magnified replicas of that original process of two centuries ago. The same outcomes: a rapid spread of misery (poverty, families and communities falling apart, human bonds tapering and being emaciated and reduced to Thomas Carlyle's 'cash nexus'), and a newly emergent 'no-man's land' (a sort of 'Wild West' like the one later to be recreated in Hollywood studios) free from binding laws and administrative supervision and only sporadically visited by itinerary judges. The original emancipation of business was followed by a long and frenetic, uphill struggle by the emergent state to invade, subdue, colonize and eventually 'normatively regulate' that land of the free-for-all, to lay institutional foundations for the 'imagined community' (dubbed 'nation') intended to take over the life-sustaining functions previously performed by households, parishes, craft guilds and other institutions that had imposed community values on business, but now fell from the weakening hands of local communities robbed of their executive power. Today we witness the 'business secession mark two': this time it is the turn of the nation-state to be cast in the status of 'households' and 'ramparts of parochialism'; to be frowned on, decried and charged as irrational relics impeding modernization and hostile to the economy.

The essence of the second secession, like that of the original one, is the divorce between power and politics. In the course of its struggle to limit the social and cultural damage of the first secession (culminating in the 'glorious thirty' years following the Second World War), the emergent modern state managed to develop institutions of politics and governance made to the measure of the postulated merger of power (*Macht, Herrschaft*) and politics inside the territorial union of nation and state. The marriage of power and politics (or rather their cohabitation inside the nation-state) now ends in divorce, with power partly evaporating upwards into cyberspace, partly flowing sideways to militantly and ruggedly apolitical markets, and partly 'subsidiarized' (forcibly, 'by decree') to the 'life politics' of newly 'enfranchised' (by decree again, by decree . . .) individuals.

The outcomes are very much the same as in the case of the original secession, only on an incomparably grander (indeed, 'radicalized') scale. Now, however, there is no equivalent in sight of the postulated 'sovereign nation-state' which might be able (or be hoped to be able) to envisage (let alone see through) a realistic prospect of taming a globalization hitherto purely negative (dismantling institutions, melting structures) and recapturing the forces running amuck in order to submit them to ethically informed and politically operated control. Thus far, at least . . . Mistaking the present 'international' (better called 'interstate') politics for (non-existent) global politics is just another expedient that serves to legitimize and 'naturalize' business anarchy (I mulled over that divorce in *In Search of Politics*, and its socio-cultural consequences in *Wasted Lives*).

All in all, we now have power free from politics, and politics devoid of power. Power is already global; politics stays pitifully local. Territorial nation-states are local 'law and order' police precincts, as well as local dustbins and garbage-removal and recycling plants for globally produced risks and problems.

Then there is migration (not necessarily in the flesh: people travel, but their abodes don't manage to stay put either). Industrial capital migrates out, away from its original localities, service capital brings people in, commercial capital travels in all directions all over the place. The prime stratifying factor in the current hierarchy of domination is facility of movement (the condition of *glebae adscripti*, of being consigned to one bit of land, is the mark/stigma of the bottom), whereas the right to decide the entitlement to mobility is the prime stake in the power struggle. Ninety per cent or more of the planet's residents stay put, in geographical terms – while those who are on the move or are already dislocated are perhaps more often made up of vagabonds (involuntary tourists) than of tourists (voluntary vagabonds).

The current wave of migration has, if anything, exposed the limitations of the nationalist expectation and determination to 'assimilate' the newcomers: to assert and preserve the priority of ethnic domicile over ethnic origin. Migration now leads on the whole to the establishment of spatially scattered diasporas, enclaves of double loyalty, using the implements offered by 'information highways' to try hard, most often successfully, to retain spiritual, and more often than not political and ideological, links with their 'native' lands. In the process, the endemic multiculturalism of the planet is brought home, so to speak – dumped into the immediate neighbourhood. The wilting of the hope of 'digesting' – converting and assimilating – the newcomers turns into another 'growth factor' of nationalist sentiments. This time, though, those sentiments mostly spawn an aggressive defence of national purity and policies of exclusion, rather than, as in the past, feeding expansive policies of incorporation and absorption.

To return to your quandary: is it possible to save the state in its present form? Or beyond that, to restore it to its past might and glory? I am inclined to answer both questions in a negative, despite the fact that at the very moment I give my answer there are scattered symptoms of influential people behaving as if positive answers were plausible and saving and/or resurrecting the state as we know it were feasible; and even despite the fact that those answers, having been given an added aura from being broadcast worldwide and reiterated endlessly by the media, may indeed acquire in many minds yet greater veracity. Myself, I've so far found no valid arguments refuting the supposition that there are no local solutions to the gravest of contemporary problems – which are by their nature global: globally produced and amenable solely to global solutions.

CRM *One of the implications of your work seems to be (correct me if I am wrong) that we have moved away from the centrality of the state: but have we really? Are we not still somehow lost in our understanding of the state? (I know I am!) It has often been said about Marx, for example, that he 'lacked a robust coherent theory of the state' (though, in the aftermath of the economic downturn, even the most conservative authors have begun to recognize the genius in Karl Marx). As for Hegel before him, he often appeared too 'romantic' and perhaps, even 'obsessed', by his teleological approach to history, and what I have regarded as an ethnocentric and logocentric[17] approach to history and law (and subsequently state-building). Postmodernism and poststructuralism did not appear to help much and did not clarify the 'big questions'.*

This century, we seem to be left with clumsy, ad hoc (and very annoying) awkward concepts, such as the 'nanny state', the 'invisible hand of the market' – and, by implication, an 'amorphous thing', the 'head', over its shoulders, invoking perhaps its rationality, but clearly in a dysfunctional relationship to its 'body'. In the twenty-first century, the state question seems as ungraspable as ever. Beyond the paradoxes described above, can we solidify the state? Should we?

Let me speculate further. The political state might have lost its centrality in the economy (the deregulating tendencies already mentioned), but it seems to retain an overwhelming centrality in certain strategic areas (including, as I have already suggested to you, the agencies of the welfare state). But also, and most importantly, the state has kept its strategic centrality in its surveillance powers. Unlike the 'ghostly state', which is conveniently absent from the banking and financial sectors (when not threatened by protectionism), the 'police state', as Britain's former head of MI5 Dame Stella Rimington referred to it recently,[18] is getting fat, very fat indeed. A police and very solid state, then: just look at the size of Big Brother (which you examined brilliantly in Society under Siege *and discussed earlier here). In the face of its power, liquidity itself begins to look like an illusion. Let's face it, Big Brother is not liquid. 'Big Brother' might have developed tentacles growing in and from the private sector, but its main drive still seems to derive from the state. Whatever happened to Ralph Miliband and Nicos Poulantzas (beyond their 'love/hate' affair) and Althusser? Are they of any relevance today? In short, Professor Bauman, do we 'bring the state back in', do we reinvent it, do we stop believing in it?*

ZB   Your guesses are as good as mine . . . And who am I to invent where Hegel or Marx, as some say, failed? Perhaps there is a chameleon quality in the phenomenon called the 'state' that renders each and any theory of it to seem either confusingly muddled or shamefully simplified? Whatever the escape route from whatever quandary you pick, you are bound to be confined by the conditions – the conditions in which choices are made are notoriously not open to choice. And by now conditions have markedly changed: the state, like the rest of the human inventions and products with which we are saddled, operates today in a world starkly different from the world in which Ralph Miliband crossed swords with Nicos Poulantzas.

Our modern world, with its compulsive and obsessive urge to 'modernize', from the beginning developed two mass industries of 'human waste' – which I attempted to analyse in more detail in the book *Wasted Lives*. One of those industries is that of order-building (which cannot do otherwise than massively produce human rejects, the 'unfit', the excluded from the realm of proper and orderly – 'normal' – society). The other, called 'economic progress', turns out huge quantities of human leftovers: humans for whom there is no place in the 'economy', no useful role to play and no opportunity to earn a living, at least in the ways defined as legal: recommended or just tolerable. The social ('welfare') state was an ambitious attempt to phase out those two industries. It was an ambitious (perhaps excessively ambitious) project of inclusion of all through phasing out and eventually eliminating the practices of social exclusion. In many respects successful, though not without its shortcomings, the social state is now itself being phased out – while the two industries manufacturing human waste are back in operation and working in full swing, the first producing 'aliens' (those 'without papers', illegal immigrants, false asylum seekers, and all sorts of other 'undesirables'), the other bringing about 'flawed consumers', and both together mass-producing the 'underclass': not a 'lower class' situated at the bottom of a class ladder, but people for whom there is no place in any social class, people cast outside the class system of 'normal society'.

The state is today unable, and/or unwilling, to promise its subjects existential security ('freedom from fear', as Franklin Delano Roosevelt famously phrased it). Gaining existential security – obtaining and retaining a legitimate and dignified place in human society and avoiding the menace of exclusion – is now left to the skills and resources of each individual on his or her own; and that means running enormous risks, and suffering the harrowing uncertainty which such tasks inevitably include. The fear the social state promised to uproot has returned, with a vengeance. Most of us, from the bottom to the top, nowadays fear the threat, however vague, of being excluded, of being proved inadequate to the challenge, of being snubbed, denied dignity and humiliated.

Politicians as much as the consumer markets are eager to capitalize on the diffuse and misty fears that saturate present-day society. The sellers of consumer goods and services advertise their commodities as foolproof remedies against the abominable sense of uncertainty and ill-defined threats. Populist movements and populist politicians pick up the task abandoned by the weakening and disappearing social state, and also by much of whatever remains of the by and large bygone socialist left. But in stark opposition to the social state, they are interested in expanding, not reducing the volume of fears; and, particularly in expanding fears of the kinds of dangers, they can be seen on TV gallantly resisting and fighting back against, and all in all protecting the nation from. The snag is that the menaces most vociferously, spectacularly and insistently displayed by the media seldom, if ever, happen to be the dangers that lie at the root of popular anxiety and fears. However successful the state might be in resisting the publicized threats, the genuine sources of anxiety, of ambient and haunting uncertainty and social insecurity, those prime causes of fear endemic to the modern capitalist way of life, will remain intact and, if anything, emerge reinforced.

In the time of globalization it is the way resentment is directed towards migrants that particularly catches the eye and the imagination, and so is politically profitable. In some perverse way, migrants represent everything that breeds anxiety and stirs up horror in the new variety of uncertainty and insecurity that has been and continues to be prompted by the mysterious, impenetrable and unpredictable 'global forces'. Migrants embody, bring 'into one's backyard', render palpable and all too visible the horrors of destroyed livelihood, enforced exile, social degradation, ultimate exclusion and relegation to a 'non-place' outside the universe of law and rights – and so they incarnate all those half-conscious or subconscious or unconscious existential fears that torment men and women in a liquid modern society. Chasing the migrants away, one rebels (by proxy) against all those mysterious global forces that threaten to visit on everybody the fate already suffered by the migrants. There is a lot of capital in that illusion that can be (and is) adroitly exploited by politicians and markets alike.

As far as the bulk of the electorate is concerned, political leaders, present and aspiring, are judged by the severity they manifest in the course of the 'security race'. Politicians try to outdo each other in promises to get tough on the culprits of insecurity – genuine or putative, but those that are near, within reach, and can be fought and defeated or at least are deemed to be conquerable and presented as such. Forza Italia or the Lega may win elections by promising to protect hard-working Lombardians against being robbed by lazy Calabrians, to defend both against newcomers who remind them of the shakiness and incurable frailty of their own positions, and to defend every and any voter against obtrusive beggars, stalkers, prowlers and muggers. The genuine, fundamental and decisive threats to human decent life and dignity will emerge from all that unscathed.

These are the reasons why the risks to which democracies are currently exposed are only partly due to the governments of states desperately seeking to legitimize their right to rule and to demand discipline – through flexing their muscles and showing their determination to stand firm in the face of endless, genuine or putative, threats to human bodies – instead of protecting their citizens' social usefulness (as they did before), their respected place in society, with insurance against exclusion, denial of dignity or humiliation. I say 'partly' because the second reason our democracy is at risk is what can only be called 'freedom fatigue', manifested in the placidity with which most of us accept the process of the step-by-step limitation of our hard-won liberties, our rights to privacy, to defence in court, to being treated as innocent until proven guilty. Laurent Bonnelli recently coined the term 'liberticide' to denote that combination of states' new and far-fetched ambitions and citizens' timidity and indifference. He asks what are the true, even if undeclared, targets of the new 'securitarian' policies: 'L'antiterrorisme contre les libertés civiles?' – antiterrorism against civil liberties?

A while ago I watched on TV thousands of passengers stranded at British airports during another 'terrorist panic', when flights were cancelled after an announcement that the 'unspeakable dangers' of a 'liquid bomb', and a worldwide plot to explode aircrafts in mid-flight, had been discovered. Those thousands grounded by cancellations lost their holidays, important business meetings, family reunions. But they did not complain! Not in the least. Neither did they protest at having been sniffed all over by dogs, kept in endless queues for security checks, submitted to body searches they would surely normally consider offensive to their dignity. On the contrary, they were jubilant: 'We have never felt so safe as now,' they kept repeating. 'We are so grateful to our authorities for their vigilance and for taking such good care of our safety!'

Keeping prisoners incarcerated for years on end without charge in camps like Guantanamo, Abu Ghraib, and perhaps in dozens more, kept secret and for that reason yet more sinister and less human, has caused occasional murmurs of protest, but hardly a public outcry, let alone an effective counteraction. We console ourselves that all those violations of human rights are aimed at 'them', not 'us' – at different kinds of humans ('between you and me, are they indeed human?!') and that those outrages will not affect us, the decent people. We have conveniently forgotten the sad conclusions of Martin Niemöller, the Lutheran pastor and a victim of Nazi persecutions: First they took the communists, he mused – but I was not a communist, so I kept silent. Then they came after trade unionists, and as I was not a trade unionist, I said nothing. Then they came after Jews, but I was not a Jew . . . And after Catholics, but I was not a Catholic . . . Then they came after me . . . But by that time there was no one left to speak up for anyone.

In an insecure world, security is the name of the game. Security is the main purpose of the game and its paramount stake. It is a value that in practice, if not in theory, dwarfs all other values and elbows them out of view – including the values dearest to 'us' while hated most by 'them', and for that reason declared the prime cause of 'their' wish to harm 'us' and 'our' duty to conquer 'them'. In a world as insecure as ours, personal freedoms of word and action, the right to privacy, access to the truth – all those things we used to associate with democracy and in whose name we still go to war – need to be trimmed or suspended. Or this is at least what the official version, confirmed by official practice, maintains.

The truth, nevertheless, is that we cannot effectively defend our freedoms here at home while fencing ourselves off from the rest of the world and attending solely to our affairs here at home . . .

There are valid reasons to suppose that on a globalized planet, where the plight of everyone everywhere determines the plight of all the others while being determined by them, one can no longer ensure freedom and democracy 'separately' – in isolation, in one country, or only in a few selected countries. The fate of freedom and democracy in each land is decided and settled on the global stage; and only on that stage can it be defended with a realistic chance of lasting success. It is no longer in the power of any singly acting state, however resourceful, heavily armed, resolute and uncompromising, to defend its chosen values at home while turning its back on the dreams and yearnings of those outside its borders. But turning our backs is precisely what we, here in Europe and other fortunate lands, seem to be doing, when we keep our riches and multiply them at the expense of the poor outside.

At its earlier stage, modernity raised human integration to the level of nations. Before it finishes its job, however, modernity needs to perform one more, yet more formidable task: raise human integration to the level of humanity, inclusive of the whole population of the planet. However hard and thorny that task may yet prove to be, it is imperative and urgent, because for a planet of universal interdependency it is, literally, a matter of (shared) life or (joint) death. A crucial condition of this task being earnestly undertaken and performed is the creation of a global equivalent of the 'social state' that completed and crowned the previous phase of modern history – that of the integration of localities and tribes into nation-states. At some point, therefore, the resurgence of the essential core of the socialist 'active utopia' – the principle of collective responsibility and collective insurance against misery and ill fortune – would be indispensable, though this time on a global scale, with humanity as a whole as its object.

At the stage the globalization of capital and commodity trade has already reached, no governments, singly or even severally, are able to balance the books – and without the books being balanced the continuation of the practices of the 'social state' that effectively cut at the roots of poverty and prevent the trend towards inequality from running wild are inconceivable. It is also difficult to imagine governments able, singly or even severally, to impose limits on consumption and raise local taxation to the levels required by the continuation, let alone further expansion, of social services. Intervention in the markets is indeed badly needed, but will it be state intervention if it does happen, and particularly if, in addition to merely happening, it also brings tangible effects?

Rather, it will be the work of non-governmental initiatives, independent of the state and perhaps even dissident. Poverty and inequality, and more generally the disastrous side-effects and 'collateral damage' of global laissez-faire cannot be effectively dealt with separately from the rest of the planet in one corner of the globe. There is no decent way in which a single or a group of territorial states may 'opt out' from the global interdependency of humanity. The 'social state' is no longer viable; only a 'social planet' can take over the functions it not so long ago tried, with mixed success, to perform.

I suspect that the vehicles likely to take us to that 'social planet' are not territorially sovereign states, but rather admittedly extra-territorial and cosmopolitan non-governmental organizations and associations; and those that reach out directly to people in need above the heads of and with no interference from the local 'sovereign' governments . . .

CRM *Another peculiar notion in our political tradition is precisely that of sovereignty. I have spent much time pondering the complexity and inconsistencies of such a concept (please forgive my own recurrent obsessions). In a long essay that I drafted in Spanish, I explored the anatomy of this strange concept which has always intrigued and fascinated me owing to its 'versatility'.[19] But in your work, particularly* Consuming Life,[20] *you took sovereignty to even more unthinkable places (well, not really – 'unthinkable' only for those of us who could not see beyond our noses). You seemed to have shown us one of the best places to look for sovereignty in our era.*

Some of the implications of your work are that it identifies more realistic 'sources' of sovereignty for our times. Reading your work, it could be suggested that in contemporary times the real 'source' and 'realm' of sovereignty is no longer – to oversimplify, if I may – the powers of government (as Machiavelli, Hobbes and Hegel had it). It is not the Divine Supremacy[21] (as Bodin had it). It is not the people (as Rousseau, Locke and Paine had it). Nor is it the constitution, as Montesquieu (and also Rousseau and Locke had it), or in law, considered as 'dictates of reason' (as Kant had it), and it is not the powers to create and abolish laws (as Austin had it). Neither will we find it, it seems, in the individual, as Kant, John Stuart Mill, Derrida, Bataille and others had it, nor in the female body, as some feminists (typically Simone de Beauvoir) had it. You really further complicated matters by stating that 'sovereignty is in the market-place'. In fact, in your view, 'the state is an executor of market sovereignty'.[22] *The new sovereigns – the market, that is – according to your book, and the financial and banking sectors, as we have painfully learnt from the events in New York and London in the autumn of 2008, have fooled us again. Where do we go from here?*

ZB What is sovereignty? Most thinkers who wish to clarify this question these days take a leaf from the prolific writings of Carl Schmitt, recently rehabilitated in the intellectual salons of Europe after long years of infamy, justly earned by his long, loyal, enthusiastic and dedicated service to one of the cruellest regimes in history. Apparently, what Carl Schmitt thought the essence of sovereignty to be, probably drawing the empirical grounding of his theory from the Nazi Führer Prinzip of which he strongly approved, has been found useful in articulating the tendency of our own powers that be. At least, this is one of permissible explanations of the amazing career of Carl Schmitt's ghost.

Carl Schmitt's idea of sovereignty, spelled out in his *Political Theology* (conceived in 1922 and recycled ten years later, with a few previously uncrossed t's crossed and the few undotted i's now dotted, into *The Concept of the Political*) was meant to be to political theory what the Book of Job has been to Judaism, and through Judaism to Christianity.

It was intended and designed to answer one of the most notoriously haunting of the born-in-Jerusalem questions: a sort of question with which the most famous of the born-in-Jerusalem ideas, the idea of a one and only god, an omnipresent and omnipotent creator of stars, mountains and seas, judge and saviour of the whole earth and the whole of humanity, could not but be born pregnant. That question would hardly have occurred elsewhere, especially to Athenians living in a world crowded with larger and smaller deities of larger or smaller nations or even townships; and it would not have occurred to the ancient, 'tribal God' Hebrews either, at least so long as their god, much like the god of the Greeks, shared the earth (even their own tiny homeland, Canaan) with uncountable gods of hostile tribes. It would not have been asked by Hebrews even in the event that their god claimed planet-wide mastery, since the Book of Job predesigned the answer before the question could be fully articulated and started haunting them in earnest. That answer, let us recall, could not be simpler: The Lord gave, the Lord took away, blessed be His name. It called for resigned obedience, but no questioning or debate; to sound convincing, it needed neither learned commentary nor profuse footnotes. The question, however, with which the idea of a one and only god was pregnant had to be born once the Hebrew prophet Jesus declared the omnipotent god to be in addition the God of Love, and once his disciple, St Paul, brought these Good Tidings to Athens – a place where questions, once asked, were expected to be answered in tune with the rules of logic. That the answer was not available off-hand shows the rather unwelcoming reception which St Paul received among garrulous and quarrelsome Athenians – and the fact that when he addressed 'the Greeks' he preferred to send his missives to the much less philosophically trained and sophisticated Corinthians . . .

In the world of the Greeks (as in the worlds of all the other countless polytheistic peoples, in which we could, with our benefit of hindsight, recognize 'postmodernists' *avant la lettre*) there was a god for every bizarre human experience and for all, life occasions, however varied, and so there was also an answer to every past and future query – and above all an explanation to every and any remembered inconsistency in divine actions, and a recipe for improvising novel yet a priori sensible explanations in the event that new inconsistencies were spotted. To pre-empt or at least to retrospectively neutralize the divine defiance of human yearning for consistency, many gods were needed. Gods aiming at cross-purposes, just as humans do; gods whose arrows could be diverted from the intended targets by the arrows released from the bows of other similarly divine archers. Gods could sustain their divine authority and keep it uncontested only jointly, in a group, the larger the better, so that the reason for a god or a goddess failing to deliver on their divine promises could be always found – in an equally divine curse cast by another one from the countless residents of the Pantheon.

All those comfortable explanations of the irritating randomness with which divine grace and condemnation were scattered – of the haphazardness of good fortune and bad luck evidently not to be bound by human piety or impiety, merits or sins – ceased to be available once the very existence of a Pantheon had been denied and the 'one and only' god laid claim to an unshared and indivisible, comprehensive and uncontested rule, decrying thereby all other deities (other tribal gods, or 'partial', 'specialist' gods) as just false pretenders. Claiming and grasping an absolute power, the God of monotheistic religion took absolute responsibility for the blessings and blows of fate, for the bad luck of the miserable as much as for the (as Goethe would say) 'long row of sunny days' of those pampered by fortune. Absolute power means no excuse for the power-holder. If the caring and protective God has no rivals, neither has He a sensible, let alone obvious, apology for the meanders of blind and deaf fate that torment humans under his rule.

The Book of Job recasts the horrifying randomness of Nature as the awe-and-tremor inspiring arbitrariness of its Ruler. It proclaims that God does not owe worshippers an account of His actions, and most certainly does not owe them an apology. As Leszek Kołakowski crisply put it, 'God owes us nothing' (neither justice as we comprehend it, nor an excuse for its absence – not even the comprehension of his own, bewilderingly volatile concept of justice). God's omnipotence includes the licence to turn and turn about, to say one thing and do another; it presumes the power of caprice and whim, the power to make miracles and to ignore the logic of necessity which lesser beings have no choice but to obey. God may strike at will, and if He refrains from striking, it is only because this is His (good, benign, benevolent, loving) will. The idea that humans may control God's actions by whatever means, including the means God himself recommended (that is, total and unconditional submission, following his commands meekly and faithfully and sticking to the letter of the Divine Law), is a blasphemy.

In stark opposition to the numb Nature of his making, the nature he creates, incarnates and personifies, God speaks and gives commands. He also finds out whether the commands have been obeyed in order to reward the obedient and punish the obstreperous. He is not indifferent to what human weaklings think and do. But just like numb Nature, he is not bound by what humans think or do. He can make exceptions – and the logic of consistency or universality are not exempt from exercising that divine prerogative. Indeed, the rule of a norm that also bounds the norm-maker is by definition irreconcilable with true sovereignty, with the absolute power to decide. To be absolute, power must include the right to neglect, suspend or abolish the norm, that is to commit acts which on the receiving side rebound as miracles. Schmitt's idea of sovereignty would engrave the preformed vision of divine order onto the ground of legislative order: 'The exception in jurisprudence is analogous to the miracle in theology . . . [T]he legal order rests on a decision and not a norm',[23] presuming that decisions are not bound to submit to norms. The power to exempt simultaneously founds God's absolute power and the fear human beings feel, continuing, incurable and born of insecurity. This is exactly what happens, according to Schmitt, when the human sovereign is no longer handcuffed by norms. Thanks to that power of exemption, humans are, as they were in the times before Law, vulnerable and uncertain.

As it blatantly violated, one by one, all the rulings of God's covenant with his 'particular treasure' among nations, the fate of Job was all but incomprehensible to the denizens of a modern state conceived as a Rechtstaat. It went against the grain of what they had been trained to believe was the meaning of the contractual obligations by which their lives were guided, and so also against the harmony and logic of civilized life. To philosophers, the story of Job was a continuous and incurable headache; it dashed their hopes of discovering, or of instilling, logic and the harmony of cause and effect in the chaotic flow of the events called 'history'. Generations of theologians broke their teeth trying in vain to bite at its mystery: like the rest of modern men and women (and everyone who memorized the message of the Book of Exodus) they had been taught to seek a rule and a norm, but the message of the Book of Job was that there is no rule and no norm that can be relied upon; more to the point, no rule or norm that the supreme power is bound by. The Book of Job anticipates Carl Schmitt's blunt verdict later that the sovereign is he who has the power of exemption. The power to impose rules stems from the power to suspend them or make them null and void.

Carl Schmitt, arguably the most clear-headed, illusion-free anatomist of the modern state and of its inbuilt totalitarian inclination, avers: 'He who determines a value, *eo ipso* always fixes a nonvalue. The sense of this determination of a value is the annihilation of the nonvalue.'[24] Determining the value draws the boundary of the normal, the ordinary, the orderly. Non-value is an exception that marks this boundary.

> The exception is that which cannot be subsumed; it defies general codification, but it simultaneously reveals a specifically juridical formal element: the decision in absolute purity . . . There is no rule that is applicable to chaos. Order must be established for juridical order to make sense. A regular situation must be created, and sovereign is he who definitely decides if this situation is actually effective . . .
> The exception does not only confirm the rule; *the rule as such lives off the exception alone.*[25]

Giorgio Agamben, the brilliant Italian philosopher, comments:

> The rule applies to the exception *in no longer applying*, in withdrawing from it. The state of exception is thus not a simple return to the chaos that preceded order but rather the situation that results from its suspension. In this sense, the exception is truly, according to its etymological root, taken outside (ex-capere), and not simply excluded.[26]

In other words, there is no contradiction between establishing a rule and making an exception. Quite the contrary, they are as close as Siamese twins, since without the power to exempt from the rule, there would be no power to make rules abide.

All this is admittedly confusing; it crassly defies commonsensical logic – yet this is a truth of power that has to be reckoned with in any attempt to comprehend its works, or to resign oneself to its incurable non-comprehensiveness. Without the Book of Job, the Book of Exodus would fail to lay foundations for God's omnipotence and Israel's obedience.

The story of Job's life told in that book was the most acute and insidious (and the least easy to repel) of all conceivable challenges to the idea of order resting on a universal norm instead of on (arbitrary) decisions. Given the contents of the toolbox and the routines currently available to reason, Job's life story was a gauntlet thrown down to the very possibility that creatures endowed with reason, and therefore plagued by an insatiable yearning for logic, might feel at home in the world. Just as the ancient astronomers desperately drew ever new epicycles to defend a heliocentric world order against the unruly evidence of the sightings in the night sky, the learned theologians quoted in the Book of Job leaned over backwards to defend the indomitable universality of the links between sin and punishment, virtue and reward, from the steadily accruing evidence of the pains inflicted on Job – in every respect an exemplary person, a God-fearing, pious creature and all in all a true paragon of virtue. To rub salt into the wound, on top of their own resounding failure to advance clinching proof for the truth of revealed explanations and salvage that truth from the acid test of Job's misfortune, the dense fog in which the allocation of good and bad luck was tightly wrapped became yet more impenetrable when God himself, provoked by Job's insistent questioning, joined the debate. God's intervention was also dismissive of and deeply humiliating to the champions of his glory. Not only did God flatly refuse all self-apology and explanation. He exposed the futility of the learned theologians' efforts and made a laughing stock of their pronouncements. He did not need their advocacy.

Job's begging: 'Tell me plainly, and I will listen in silence: show me where I have erred . . . Why hast thou made me thy butt, and why have I become thy target?' (Job 6: 24; 7: 20) waited in vain for God's answer. Job expected that much: 'Indeed this I know for the truth, that no man can win his case against God. If a man chooses to argue with him, God will not answer one question in a thousand . . . Though I am right, I get no answer . . . Blameless, I say . . . But it is all one; therefore I say: He destroys blameless and wicked alike' (Job 9: 2–3; 9: 15, 22).

Job expected no answer to his complaint, and at least on this point he was evidently in the right. God ignored his question, and questioned instead Job's right to ask: 'Brace yourself and stand like a man; I will ask questions, and you shall answer. Dare you deny that I am just or put me in the wrong that you may be right? Have you an arm like God's arm, can you thunder with a voice like his?' (Job 40: 6–9). God dismissed Job's questions not on substance, but on formality. Job's question was inadmissible because the questioner had no right to question. All the matter boiled down to was who had the power, and so also the right, to ask questions. God's own questions pre-empted Job's conceivable responses. Job knew only too well that he had no arm or voice to match God's, and so by implication he was aware that it was not God who owed him explanations, but it was he who owed God an apology (let's note that, on Holy Scripture's authority, it was God's questions, not Job's, that came 'out of the tempest' – that archetype of all other blows known to be immune to all begging for mercy and to strike at random).

Something of which Job might have been as yet unaware was that in centuries to come all the earthly pretenders to a God-like omnipotence would find the unpredictability and haphazardness of their thunder to be the most effective of their weapons – precisely because it was by far the most awesome and most terrorizing; and that whoever might wish to steal the rulers' thunder must first disperse the fog of uncertainty wrapped round it and recast randomness into regularity, the state of anomie (an absence of norms, or a fluidity of the limits to normative regulation) into a norm. But then Job could not anticipate that; he was not a creature of modernity.

As long as it confronted humans in the guise of an omnipotent yet benevolent God, Nature was a mystery that defied human comprehension: how indeed to square God's benevolence cum omnipotence with the profusion of evil in a world He himself had designed and set in motion? The solution to that quandary most commonly on offer – that the natural disasters visited upon humanity were so many just punishments visited upon moral sinners by God, that supreme ethical legislature, supreme court of justice and executive arm of moral law rolled into one – would not account for what in the budding modern mind stood for stark evidence, that, as summed up laconically by Voltaire in his poem composed to commemorate the 1755 Lisbon earthquake and fire, 'l'innocent, ainsi que le coupable/subit également ce mal inévitable' (roughly: the innocent, as much as the guilty, are subject to that inescapable evil). The mind-boggling quandary haunted the philosophes of emergent modernity just as it did the generations of theologians. The evident profligacy of evil in the world could not be recon-ciled with the combination of benevolence and omnipotence imputed to the world's maker and supreme manager.

The contradiction could not be resolved; it could be only taken off the agenda by what Max Weber described as the *Entzäuberung* ('disenchantment') of Nature, that is, stripping Nature of its divine disguise, which he chose as the true birth act of the 'modern spirit': that is, of the hubris grounded in the new 'we can do it, we shall do it, we will do it' attitude of daring, self-assurance and determination. In a sort of penalty for the inefficacy of obedience, prayer and the practice of virtue (the three instruments recommended as certain to evoke the desirable responses from the benevolent and omnipotent divine subject), Nature was stripped of subjecthood, and so denied the very capacity of choosing between benevolence and malice. All their previous failures nowithstanding, humans could go on hoping to ingratiate themselves in God's eyes, amassing yet more evidence to prove their innocence, protesting God's verdicts and arguing their cases – but trying to debate and bargain with 'disenchanted' Nature in the hope of currying its graces was evidently pointless. As it happened, however, Nature had been stripped of subjectivity not in order to restore or salvage the subjectivity of God, but to pave the way to deification of His human subjects.

With humans put in charge, the uncertainty conditioned by Nature and the 'cosmic fears' fed by uncertainty did not vanish, of course, and Nature, denuded of its divine disguise, appeared no less tremendous, menacing and terror-inspiring than before; but what prayers failed to accomplish, science-supported techne, targeted on dealing with blind and dumb nature, though not with omniscient and speaking God, surely would, once it had accumulated enough skills to do things and used them to have things done. One could now expect the randomness and unpredictability of Nature to be but a temporary irritant, and believe that the prospect of forcing Nature into obedience to the human will to be but a matter of time: natural disasters might (and should, and would) be subjected to the same treatment as that designed for social ills – the kinds of adversities that, with due skill and effort, could be exiled from the human world and their return barred. The discomforts caused by Nature's antics would eventually be dealt with as effectively as the calamities brought about by human malice and wantonness could, at least in principle, be dealt with. Sooner or later, all threats, natural and moral alike, would become predictable and preventable, obedient to the power of reason; how soon it would happen depended solely on the determination with which the powers of human reason were deployed. Nature would become just like those other aspects of the human condition that are evidently human-made and so in principle manageable and able to be 'corrected'. As Immanuel Kant's categorical imperative implied, by deploying reason, our inalienable endowment, we can raise the moral judgement and the kind of behaviour that would follow it to the rank of universal natural law.

This is how it was hoped human affairs would develop at the start of the modern era and through a good part of its history. As present experience suggests, they developed in the opposite direction. Rather than promoting reason-guided behaviour to the rank of natural law, it degraded its consequences to the level of irrational and morally indifferent nature. Natural catastrophes did not become more like 'principally manageable' moral misdeeds. It was, on the contrary, the lot of immorality to become or to be revealed as ever more similar to the erstwhile natural catastrophes: hazardous, incomprehensible, unpredictable, unpreventable, and immune to human reason and wishes. Disasters brought about by human actions nowadays descend from an opaque world, strike at random, in places impossible to anticipate, and escape or defy the kinds of explanation that set human actions apart from all other events: explanations by motive or purpose. Above all, the calamities caused by human immoral actions appear ever more unmanageable in principle.

This is what Carl Schmitt found in the world he was born in and grew into. A world divided between secular states that, according to a retrospective summary scripted by Ernst-Wolfgang Böckenförde, 'lived off preconditions which they could not themselves guarantee'.[27] The modern vision of a 'powerful, rational state', a 'state of real substance', 'standing above society and remaining immune from sectarian interests',[28] a state capable of claiming the standing of the precondition or determinant of social order, the standing once occupied by God but now vacated, seemed to dissolve and evaporate in the reality of sectarian strife, revolutions, powers incapable of acting and societies reluctant to be acted upon.

The ideas that assisted at the birth of the modern era hoped and promised to eliminate and extirpate once and for all the erratic twists and turns of contingent fate, together with the resulting opacity and unpredictability of the human condition and prospects that had marked the rule of Jerusalem God, and which Jerusalem God, the master and guardian of the 'chosen people', refused to correct, 'rejected the exception in every form'.[29] Those ideas rested on the hope and promise of an alternative, solid and reliable precondition of social order in an indubitably human invention and human-made artifice, the constitutional liberal state, which was expected to replace the capricious finger of divine providence with the invisible, yet steady and reliable hand of an omniscient and omnipotent market. The hope has been met with abominable failure, however, while the promises have proved to hang anywhere except within the reach of the states they envisaged. In his garb of the modern 'powerful and rational' state, Jerusalem God found himself in Athens, that messy playground of mischievous and scheming gods – where, to follow Plato, the gods would be dying from laughter at hearing his pretence to a 'one and only' status, while (to be on the safe side) making sure that their quivers were constantly full of arrows. In so far as the gospels of the theorists and panegyrists of the modern state followed the lead of Jerusalem God, stoutly refusing recognition to other pretenders to divine status, an updated version of the Book of Job was obviously needed – and missed.

But the happy-go-lucky Athenian reconciliation to the plurality of the obstreperously uncomplaisant and quarrelsome gods (the kind of settlement brought to its logical conclusion by the Roman practice of adding new busts to the Pantheon with every new territorial conquest) would not do either for the hapless residents of the modern world, that precarious arrangement founded on the (un)holy trinitarian alliance of state, nation and territory. In this modern world there might be, as in Athens or Rome, many divinities, but places where they could meet in peace and fraternize, a Parthenon or a Pantheon designed for their affable conviviality, were conspicuously absent. Their encounter would inevitably make any meeting place into a battlefield and a front line, since following the principles originated by Jerusalem God each triune formation would claim an absolute, inalienable and indivisible sovereignty in its own domain. The world into which Schmitt was born was not the polytheistic world of the Athenians or Romans, but a world of *cuius regio eius religio* (with the ruler setting the religion), of an uneasy cohabitation of viciously competitive, intolerant, self-proclaimed 'one and only' gods. The world populated by states in search of nations and nations in search of states could be polytheistic (and would be likely to remain so for some time still), but each part of it defended tooth and nail its own prerogative of monotheism (religious, secular, or both – as in the case of modern nationalism).

That principle and that intention were to be recorded in the statutes of the League of Nations and restated, with yet greater emphasis, in the rules and regulations of the United Nations, instructed to uphold with all its (genuine or putative) powers the sacrosanct right of every member state to its own uncompromising sovereignty over the fate and lives of its subjects at home. The League of Nations, and later the United Nations, wished to pull out the nation-states, bent on indivisible sovereignty, from the battlefield, their hitherto normal and tested ground of cohabitation and reciprocal genocide, and place them instead and keep them at a round table, prompting them to converse and negotiate; it aimed to lure the warring tribes to Athens with the promise to make their tribal, Jerusalem-style gods still firmer, more indisputable and unchallenged.

Carl Schmitt saw through the futility of that intention. The charges that can (and should) be laid against him are the charge of liking what he saw, the yet more serious charge of embracing it enthusiastically, and a truly unforgivable charge of earnestly trying to do his best to raise the pattern he distilled from the practices of twentieth-century Europe to the rank of the eternal law of all and any politics; the charge of conferring on that pattern the distinction of the one and only attribute of the political process that elides and transcends even the sovereign's power of exemption, and the only one that might set a limit to the sovereign's power of decision – a limit that the sovereign can ignore only at his own mortal peril. These are well-justified charges; a charge of imperfect vision, on the other hand, would be groundless if it were aimed at Schmitt. It ought be laid instead at the door of those who saw otherwise and whose vision Schmitt set about correcting . . .

If you put together Schmitt's assertion that he is sovereign who decides on the exception (more importantly, decides arbitrarily, 'decisionistic and personalistic elements'[30] being most crucial in Schmitt's concept of sovereignty), and his insistence that the distinction which defines 'the political' aspect in human actions and motives, an opposition to which those actions and motives can be in fact reduced, 'is that between friend and enemy',[31] then what follows is that the substance and the trademark of every and any holder of sovereignty and/or every and any sovereign agency is 'association and dissociation'; more exactly, association-through-dissociation, the deployment of 'dissociation' in the production and servicing of 'association': naming the 'enemy' that needs to be 'dissociated', so that 'friends' may remain 'associated'. In a nutshell, pinpointing, setting apart, labelling and declaring war on the enemy. In Schmitt's vision of sovereignty, association is inconceivable without dissociation, order without expulsion and extinction, creation without destruction. The strategy of destruction for the sake of order-building is the defining feature of (every and any, as Schmitt insists) sovereignty.

The naming of the enemy is a 'decisionistic' and 'personalistic' act since 'the political enemy need not be morally evil or aesthetically ugly'; indeed, the 'enemy' needs not be guilty of hostile deeds or intentions – it is sufficient that 'he is the other, the stranger, something different and alien'.[32] Given that politics consists in the act of naming the enemy and fighting the enemy, and the decisionistic nature of sovereignty, it must be clear that someone becomes 'the other' and 'the stranger', and ultimately 'an enemy', at the end, not at the starting point, of the sovereign's political action. Indeed, an 'objectivity' of enmity (the condition of 'being an enemy' being determined by the enemy's own attributes and actions) would go against the grain of a sovereignty that boils down to the right of making exceptions. An enemy defined by its own malice aforethought and its own hostile initiatives would be dangerously similar in its effects to a covenant equally binding Jehovah and the people of Israel: something as unacceptable to modern sovereigns as it was to the jealous and vengeful God of the Book of Job. At least thus spake Carl Schmitt, after taking a close look at the practices of the most decisive and unscrupulous seekers of sovereignty of his time; perhaps after also noticing the 'totalitarian inclination' endemic, as Hannah Arendt suggested, to all modern forms of state power.

Human vulnerability and uncertainty is the foundation of all political power. Powers claim authority and obedience by promising their subjects effective protection against these two banes of the human condition. In the Stalinist variety of totalitarian power, that is in the absence of the market-produced randomness of the human condition, vulnerability and uncertainty had to be artificially produced and reproduced by the political power itself deploying political means. It was more than sheer coincidence that random terror was unleashed on a massive scale in communist-ruled Russia to coincide with a folding up of the last residues of the NEP (the New Economic Policy reinviting the market in after its banishment in the years of the 'war communism').

In most modern societies the vulnerability and insecurity of existence and the need to pursue life purposes under conditions of acute and unredeemable uncertainty was assured from the start by the exposure of life pursuits to the vagaries of market forces. Apart from protecting market freedoms and occasionally helping to resuscitate the dwindling vigour of market forces, political power had no need to engage directly in the production of insecurity. In demanding subjects' discipline and observance of law, it could perversely, though credibly, rest its legitimacy on the promise to mitigate the extent of the already existing vulnerability and uncertainty of its citizens: to limit the harm and damage perpetrated by the free play of market forces, to shield the vulnerable against terminal or excessively painful blows, and to insure all citizens against at least some risks among the many that free, catch-as-catch-can competition necessarily entails. Such legitimation found its ultimate expression in the self-definition of the modern form of government as a 'welfare state'.

That formula of political power has, however, started to recede into the past with the advent of the 'liquid' phase of modernity, with its attendant forms of governance and strategies of domination. 'Welfare state' institutions were progressively dismantled and phased out, while restraints previously imposed on business activities and on the free play of market competition and its dire consequences were removed one by one. The protective functions of the state were tapered down to focus on a small minority of the unemployable and invalid, though even that minority tended to be reclassified from an 'issue of social care' into a 'problem of law and order': an incapacity to participate in the market game tended to be increasingly criminalized. The state washed its hands of the vulnerability and uncertainty arising from the logic (or illogicality) of the free market – a condition now redefined as a private fault and a private affair, a matter for individuals to deal with and cope with using the resources in their private possession. As Ulrich Beck memorably put it, individuals were now expected to seek biographical solutions to systemic contradictions.[33]

These new trends have a side-effect: they sap the foundations on which the state's power, claiming a crucial role in fighting the vulnerability and uncertainty haunting its subjects, increasingly

rested in modern times. The widely noted growth of political
apathy, the erosion of political interests and loyalties ('no more
salvation by society', as Peter Drucker famously put it, or 'there
is no such thing as society', there are only individuals and families,
as Margaret Thatcher equally bluntly declared), and a massive
retreat of the population from participation in institutionalized
politics all testified to a crumbling of the established foundations
of state power.

Having rescinded its previous programmatic therapeutic posture
towards the consequences of market-produced insecurity, and
having on the contrary proclaimed the perpetuation and intensi-
fication of that insecurity to be the mission of all political power
caring for the well-being of its subjects, the contemporary state
must seek other, non-economic varieties of vulnerability and
uncertainty on which to rest its legitimacy. That alternative seems
to have been recently located (perhaps most spectacularly, but by
no means exclusively, by the US administration) in the issue of
personal safety: threats to human bodies, possessions and habitats
arising from criminal activities, anti-social conduct by the 'underclass' and, most recently, global terrorism. Unlike the insecurity
born of the market, which is if anything all too visible and obvious
for comfort, that alternative insecurity through which it is hoped
to restore the state's lost monopoly of redemption must be artificially beefed up, or at least highly dramatized, to inspire sufficient
'official fear' and at the same time overshadow and relegate to a
secondary position the economically generated insecurity about
which the state administration can and intends to do nothing.

Unlike in the case of the all-too-obvious horrors of market-
generated harm to social standing, self-dignity and livelihood, it
needs great effort for the extent of the dangers to personal safety
to be presented and perceived in the darkest of colours, so that
(much as in the Stalinist political regime) the non-materialization
of threats can be ap-plauded as an extraordinary event, a result
of the vigilance, care and goodwill of state organs. No wonder
this is the heyday of the power of exemption, states of emergency
and the nomination of enemies (no wonder the loyal Nazi Carl
Schmitt has been returned to intellectual favours). It is a moot
question whether the power to exempt is an eternal essence of all
sovereignty, and whether the selection and pillorying of enemies
is the extemporal substance of 'the political'. There is, however,

little doubt that nowadays the muscles of the powers that be are flexed in the pursuit of those two activities as hardly ever before.

CRM *Let me bring into the discussion the question of human rights. You just touched on the League of Nations. On this issue, it is difficult to ignore the ethnocentric foundations upon which the latter and the United Nations, as we know it today, were built: that had dramatic consequences for postcolonial geopolitics, particularly regarding the rights to self-determination and the right to autonomy of indigenous nations in Latin America[34] – the recently adopted United Nations Declaration on the Rights of Indigenous Peoples (2007)[35] representing, however, substantial and favourable changes. This next question, which further explores your reflections on sovereignty and its relevance to our young century, is divided into three parts: What future do you envisage for the UN system in the aftermath of a financial crisis which was caused, among other reasons, precisely by the erosion of the sovereignty of the nation-state in the terms discussed earlier? If the already complex issues of sovereignty have been made worse by globalization, what is the future for the international community? What can the remains of the state, in the age of deregulation, do to enforce international human rights law? What are, in your view, the most pressing issues on the human rights agenda when the UN's credibility is in disrepute after the war in Iraq, and given that human rights doctrine increasingly appears to be exploited, according to some authors, as a justification for political, military and economic power?[36] How can one approach human rights doctrine dilemmas beyond the relativist/universalist debates?[37] What is the best way to approach the conflict between universalistic and relativist approaches when often the tension between them appears to be at the heart of many violent conflicts today?*

And finally, in 2008 we commemorated the sixtieth anniversary of the Universal Declaration of Human Rights. A number of changes in the UN narrative in the decades subsequent to its proclamation gave rise to conflicting approaches[38] and new movements (including the so-called 'emerging human rights').[39] The question here is, do you envisage the Universal Declaration having more, or less, relevance compared with the impact it had when it was first written in the aftermath of the Holocaust?

Is the former going to be held dear to us, as it was in the last century, or is it going to represent 'the last' lost treasure of modernity, the final casualty of liquidity?

ZB   At the time of the First World War, a war prompted by the conflicting interests of European imperial metropolises, waged and conducted between European powers albeit fought on the worldwide stage, 'sovereignty' was a demanding notion reflecting the European capacity (and even more the European ambition) to treat the globe as its playground. The idea of sovereignty having been cut to the measure of the extant or aspiring empires, only a few states could claim it and fewer still could have their claim recognized. Just compare the compact size of the League of Nations building in Geneva with the overflowing UN compound in New York, or the lists of national dialling codes half a page long in the old telephone directories with the length of the list of countries that every internet trading company asks you to choose from. To be recognized as a sovereign power, a state, a population needed, in credible theory if not in convincing practice, to base its claim to political sovereignty on the tripod of economic, military and cultural self-sufficiency; in none of these three areas would any of the 200 odd members of the UN pass the test of autarky. The present-day proliferation of 'politically independent' units follows the drastic lowering of the standards required to be reached before the recognition of sovereignty is granted by the 'international community' (whatever that bizarre expression may be meant to mean).

The protection not of human rights but of 'collective security' was the declared purpose and task of the League of Nations. By 'collective security' was meant the preservation of the status quo; and 'status quo' meant in its turn the division of the globe into a few dozen sovereign entities, each secure in its own borders against the trespassing or annexing appetites of other, stronger entities. We may say that the entities that had had their territorial sovereignty already recognized agreed to collectively promote and defend that principle of the planet's division into sovereign plots. If no borders had been violated, no territorial aggression committed, no internal sovereignty of a state undermined or threatened, the League of Nations would have been seen as acquitting itself fully in its statutory obligations. Each established member of the

League of Nations was accorded the role of the one and only legitimate plenipotentiary and spokesman for the population residing within its state borders. What happened to that population and how it was treated by the powers that be was each member's 'internal affair' and no concern of the League; indeed, this was an integral, inseparable, perhaps even the axial part of the idea of state sovereignty that the League of Nations was called into life in order to protect tooth and nail.

The heart (indeed, the defining trait) of politics, if one believes Carl Schmitt (arguably the most sober and outspoken synthesizer of the political doxa of the solid modern era), was naming an enemy; it did not matter whether the chosen enemy was practising hostility or contemplating hostile actions; the sole thing that mattered was that it had been decreed an enemy at the sovereign's behest. It did not matter either whether the enemy resided outside or inside the borders. The sovereign, exercising his 'decisionist' prerogative (that is, not obliged to refer his steps to other factors by way of explaining why were they taken), was free to appoint an enemy at will, the sole (advised, though not obligatory) consideration being the expediency of the choice made. Appointing an enemy within reach and within one's power to tackle seems to be the very epitome of expediency. That circumstance boded ill for some people, though for whom exactly it was left to the sovereign to decide. And with 'collective security' taking care of genuine or putative enemies outside, the sovereign could all the more thoroughly and profitably focus on internal ones in his effort to beef up the obedience of subjects to a frenzy of enthusiastic support.

Hannah Arendt flawlessly spotted the endemic ambiguity of the winged phrase of one of the constitutional documents of the modern era: 'The rights of man and citizen'. Does the citizen enjoy rights thanks to being human, or vice versa? Can human rights be had and enjoyed only if the human in question is also a citizen? The big question (implied, but unanswered, left open, abandoned to the 'decisionist' practice of sovereigns) was the status of a human who was not a citizen; and on a planet mobilizing its resources and energy for the sake of preserving the territorial division and separation of sovereignties, being a 'citizen' could only mean being a citizen of one of the sovereign states. To imitate the rhetorical figures favoured by Carl Schmitt and by

Giorgio Agamben, his most influential present-day interpreter, we may say that rights intervened in the status of stateless humans solely by being withdrawn or denied. For all practical intents and purposes, in the League of Nations era the concept of 'human rights' was an empty term unless it referred to rights accorded (and by the same token rights that could be taken back) by a sovereign state.

In this sense the Universal Declaration of Human Rights – signed thanks to the shocking impact, still fresh in the memory, of the revolting discovery of how far a sovereign could go in his freedom to appoint enemies and to decide their fate – was a genuine novelty; it remained, however, a dead letter (a non-enforced and unenforceable declaration of intent) for most of its history. Sixty years later it still lacks regular, established institutional support. As a matter of fact, it can count on no support except for volatile and as a rule short-lived explosions of public condemnation of its violators and compassion for the victims of violence, and for ad hoc assizes improvised mostly to lock a stable from which a horse has already bolted – both 'supports' running out of steam well before finishing the assigned task. Its future fate depends on progress or lack of progress in resolving the more general issue of genuinely global institutions capable of extending effective control over the social and political consequences of hitherto rampant and unregulated globalization ('negative' globalization, as I call it: globalization limited to the forces that specialize in ignoring borders and lines of communal self-defence and in violating or by-passing locally established and binding laws).

As far as the advance of globalization is concerned, politics lies far behind the economy, all economies – legal, illegal and shadowy. The Atlantic Charter signed by Roosevelt and Churchill in Placentia Bay, Newfoundland, naming four principles on which the planetary order was to be grounded, and the UN Charter, aimed at putting in place the instruments promoting those principles, envisaged no limitations to the state's sovereignty and therefore no revision of the prewar status of human rights (the only form in which a sort of universal human right appears in the Atlantic Charter is the entitlement of people of every country to select the form of government they prefer; the emphasis here falls on the indivisible sovereignty of each country, however, with other powers desisting from interference). The United Nations was briefed from the start to observe the sanctity of state sovereignty and fight (better still, prevent) its violation from the outside, defined a priori as an act of aggression.

The structures it was hoped to install and the procedures expected to be established in the global space to sustain the planet-wide order were not global in their nature but 'international' (interstate, more precisely): the economic departures after the war soon rendered such structures and procedures woefully inadequate to confront and handle, let alone control and direct, the fast globalizing commodity, finance and labour markets. The two realities (political and economic) acted ever more blatantly in opposite directions. If the UN tried to reinforce and fortify state power, global economic forces promoted, whether by design or default, severe limitations on the state, and so obliquely on national sovereignty (limitations variously codenamed 'deregulation', 'privatization', or 'freedom of trade and capital transfers'). A side-effect of the pressures of global economic forces was a truly spectacular proliferation of formally sovereign states: a tendency that yet further fragmented the cast of players in the ongoing drama of 'international politics', yet further diminished the chances that politics could measure up to the capacities of global finances, and gave yet more rope to global economic forces.

We are, by and large, still in much the same situation of an economy free from political control confronting politics stripped of much of its power – though the recent collapse of the global economic colossus revealed the clay from which its legs were made and the sand on which their castle of splendour and opulence has been built. The reduction of the role of political entities to that of police precincts monitoring and repairing routine order in local neighbourhoods was not after all such a good thing either for those who thought, when they were promoting it, they were acting with the best interests of stockholders, and more generally of profit-making, in mind.

It remains to be seen whether the economic giants seeking salvation from the previously derided 'state bureaucracy' will go down in the history books as the global capital's Canossa, or as another shrewd attempt to reach in to the areas which capital's previous self-administered practices had failed to conquer and exploit. It is, as before, the 'ordinary folks' who are now expected to replenish the bottomless coffers of the global corporations; as they did not do that in sufficient measure when they were just tempted and seduced to do so, perhaps they will do it on a more satisfactory scale when they are forced by the state to mortgage their and their children's future to a degree they wouldn't have accepted even if had been tempted and cajoled by the cleverest of PR agencies.

International, you suggest, human rights . . . Those, by and large, are in operation, though not without a huge margin of lurid (if covered up in shame) cases of their violation by powers that believe they can afford it and get away with it (as in the case of the undisclosed numbers of prisoners captured and held without trial and charge in similarly undisclosed improvised jails, camps and torture chambers built, commissioned or hired in various parts of the globe by the CIA or the Pentagon in the frame of the 'war on terrorism'). Those exceptions apart, humans may by and large count on humane treatment everywhere in the world, at least on the degree of humanity with which the natives are treated. Embassies and consulates are expected to see to it and demand that this is done in relation to citizens of the countries they represent. Just as in the matter of the preservation of state sovereignty previously discussed, the 'universality' of human rights is protected and hoped to be assured by the solidarity of governments in doing to others what they would wish others to do to them. There is nothing, however, to prevent such solidarity from being broken unilaterally, if a country was able to bet on its citizens being properly treated in foreign countries without reciprocating that courtesy.

This is, however, as far as 'international human rights' go. But even in such a limited volume those rights are not granted and recognized unconditionally. To have the right to expect humane treatment, foreigners need to hold a valid passport certifying their citizenship of a recognized state, but also be exempted from being barred from entry by the authorities established to perform the task of controlling cross-border traffic. In this area, intergovernmental solidarity grinds to a halt. There is no 'international symmetry' in secretly locking up foreigners without a criminal charge and showing them the door. Governments that practise it would most certainly raise an outcry, and call for punitive sanctions in the name of the 'international human rights', if their citizens were accorded similar treatment in the countries from which their prisoners arrived. When writing these words, I came across a short item in the *New York Times* of 27 December 2008, one of oodles of notes with a similar content you'd find in daily papers in the US and indeed all around Europe, squeezed somewhere between the latest news from the bedrooms of celebrities on the showbusiness stage and the latest soundbites from the latest 'international' gathering of ones on the political stage. Let me quote a fragment of it:

> CENTRAL FALLS, R.I. – Few in this threadbare little mill town gave much thought to the Donald W. Wyatt Detention Facility, the maximum-security jail beside the public ball fields at the edge of town. Even when it expanded and added barbed wire, Wyatt was just the backdrop for Little League games, its name stitched on the caps of the team it sponsored . . . Then people began to disappear: the leader of a prayer group at St. Matthew's Roman Catholic Church; the father of a second grader at the public charter school; a woman who mopped floors in a Providence courthouse. After days of searching, their families found them locked up inside Wyatt – only blocks from home, but in a separate world . . . In this mostly Latino city, hardly anyone had realized that in addition to detaining the accused drug dealers and mobsters everyone heard about, the jail held hundreds of people charged with no crime – people caught in the nation's crackdown on illegal immigration. Fewer still knew that Wyatt was a portal into an expanding network of other jails, bigger and more remote, all propelling detainees toward deportation with little chance to protest.

But let me point out that originally, as articulated in the Universal Declaration, the concept of 'human rights' was invested with a yet more profound meaning, one that to this day remains a postulate and in no way binds powers endowed with the right 'to make exception', to execute a law through its withdrawal or suspension. That more profound meaning refers to human rights as deriving from an inalienable 'natural law' that applies to all humans, including those who have been banished, stripped of citizenship or forced to flee from their countries under the threat to their lives; and to human rights that override the prerogatives of governments drawn from the idea of 'sovereignty': prerogative to deny to their own subjects the dignity and respect owed to all human beings. I doubt whether such a deeper understanding of human rights, let alone the practice that such an understanding would demand, stands much chance of becoming a universal rule as long as we are obliged to speak of international (interstate, intergovernmental) human rights instead of global (planetary) ones – tacitly referring to an agreement ratified by state governments instead of calling into action the (thus far non-existent) global political and legal institutions resourceful enough to make the word flesh.

CRM   *Most of us will never forget where we were and what we were doing when, nearly a decade ago, the events of 9/11 took place. The terrorist attacks on North American cities in September 2001 have become engraved on the collective memory and collective 'imaginary' of an entire generation, forging our perception of politics for the first part of the twenty-first century. Most of us became paralyzed with disbelief and horror; many, however, soon realized that, among the consequences of such tragic incidents, there could be a subsequent assault on our civil liberties by those very institutions of modernity that had promised to protect them, while others anticipated the rise of a 'fear industry' and a 'fear culture'.[40] And the intuition was not wrong: soon after the attacks, the US and Britain introduced new legislation that, one way or another, would result in the infringement of well-established civil liberties.[41] We know that only a small minority of extremist voices would have condoned or supported the attacks, which were otherwise widely condemned across the world. But the question I ask you now is, in condemning international terrorism and rendering it morally and politically unacceptable – which it most certainly is – have we lost sight of the emergence of new forms of authoritarianism?*

Is Max Weber's concept of the 'monopoly of the legitimate use of violence'[42] relevant to understanding the question of terrorism today? Is it analytically correct to say that, with the displacement of international terrorism from the periphery (in the 1970s) to the centre of world politics during the last decade, the state can be seen as having its monopoly threatened? Are we witnessing a battle for the monopoly of 'legitimized coercion' (between the periphery and the centre)? Is the figure of 'state terrorism' sociologically and epistemologically valid? Is this a legitimate, useful and pertinent question in today's paranoid atmosphere? Is the 'privatization of violence' (a new industry 'selling security', with

the increasing proliferation of 'enforcement' and 'personal secu-
rity' companies, from Iraq to car parks in Britain and neighbour-
hoods in Latin American countries, threatened by 'organized
crime') part of the equation in the battle for the monopoly of the
'legitimate use of violence'? If the state monopoly is threatened,
what will the consequences be for recession? Or is the latter going
to be reorganized as part of the former – it has already been
regarded by the new US National Intelligence as a matter of
'national security'.[43]

ZB Max Weber treated the state's monopoly of coercion (the
application of force) as a postulate defining the uniqueness of the
state among the other social institutions. The monopoly of coercion was accordingly the state's ambition, but hardly ever a reality.
It meant the denial of legitimacy of all and any coercion to anybody
unless they were commanded or licensed to use it at the behest of
state organs. All other uses of coercion were by the same token
defined as violence, and treated as a punishable crime. To put it
simply, the demand of a state monopoly of coercion defined the
right of the state to draw a binding line separating coercion (i.e.
legitimate violence) from violence (i.e. illegitimate coercion). The
derivative was the right of the state to decide which specific use
of force was a case of coercion exercised in the service of the
introduction or maintenance of law and order, and which was on
the contrary an act undermining law and order, whether intention-
ally or in its consequences. In practice, the usurpation of the sole
right to make that distinction was a feature confined by and large
to the modern state – a trait in fact distinguishing the modern state
from its premodern varieties (a circumstance described by Norbert
Elias, albeit in somewhat misleading cultural rather than political
terms, as the 'civilizing process').

For a large part of the modern era the corollary of the above
was an assumption that the legal application of force (that is,
coercion as distinct from violence) is a function to be initiated,
performed and administered solely by state organs, subject to
political supervision. It has been, however, together with some
other orthodox functions of the modern state, delegated by the
state to private (commercial) agencies in many of its crucial parts,
the most spectacular cases thus far having been private prisons
or internment camps, private investigating and interrogating

agencies, private parole services and 'private police' in the shape of armed guards.

There is a more profound, largely subterranean process, however, eroding not only the right of the state to draw and police the line separating coercion from violence, but the very clarity of that distinction: growing contention about what constitutes legitimate rights, part and parcel of the kind of 'law and order' that is to be defended, and what is an illegitimate and unjustifiable imposition. That other process is an aspect of the presently ongoing change in the nature of human bonds and the bundles of rights and duties that constitute their contents. Is the provision of sexual services a husband's right and the wife's duty? How far do parents' prerogatives to interfere with their children's spirits and bodies extend? What are the limits to the treatment by bosses of employees? The new notions of 'marital rape', 'date rape', 'sexual abuse of children', 'sexual harrassment in the workplace' testify to the extent and intensity of that process. In daily life and daily interaction, the notions of coercion and violence, uses of force supported by norms or to be condemned, duties and unwarranted enforcement, are now thrown into a melting pot. They are all objects of contestation; in fact, of continual 'reconnaissance battles' aimed at exploring the degree of fixity and firmness of received concepts of norms, rights and obligations, of the strength and determination of the forces in defence of them continuing to be binding – as well as the limits to which a renegotiation of norms, rights and duties might be pushed, and to the size of new entitlements that could be, with due effort, gained as a result. The omnipresence and intensity of such reconnaissance battles pursuing a reclassification of certain forms of conduct from the category of 'normal and to be expected' to 'violent and condemnable' account in large part for the present popular impression of a steep increase in violence.

Quite a different matter is the overall erosion of the territorial sovereignty of states, also affecting the binding force and effectiveness of the lines drawn by the state to separate coercion and violence (more generally, legitimate and illegitimate, that is punishable, conduct), particularly in relation to the comparatively mobile, though also the most consequential, sectors of society. For instance, according to the latest report by the highest Treasury authorities in Britain, the sum total of taxes avoided/escaped by the largest (richest) companies is calculated to be between 3.7 and 13.7 billion pounds. The width of the eventual range bears eloquent testimony to the fogginess of the legally prescribed distinction between the legally right and the legally wrong. The effectiveness of state decisions tends to be severely diminished nowadays when they can be countermanded by the facility to escape their execution. For most of the companies investigated, merely shifting the registered abode of the headquarters to an offshore address seems to have been sufficient to render their legally prescribed duty null and void; coercing those companies to pay taxes could be, as a result, contested in the courts as unlawful violence . . .

Finally, the question of the diminishing defensibility of territorial frontiers, related to the falling importance of space in matters of security. Global terrorism exploits that particular development to great effect, in its effort to keep 'the enemy' in a state of constant alert, financially ruinous in the long run and catastrophic for the personal security against violence, and yet more importantly the personal freedoms, that modern states promised to provide and protect. However seminal and shocking the advent of global terrorism might be, it does not necessarily collide with the principle of the 'state monopoly of violence' in any truly novel way. That principle (a postulate, I repeat, never completely fulfilled, a horizon never truly reached) was throughout the modern era counteracted in a great number of ways and assaulted (in practice, if not in theory) by a great number of forces. For Max Weber, cosmopolitan terrorists would be just one more force that by its very presence adds momentum to the state-proclaimed and pursued imperative . . .

Part Two

Conversation IV

Modernity, postmodernity and genocide: from decimation and annexation to 'collateral damage'

Citlali Rovirosa-Madrazo *In* Modernity and the Holocaust *(1989), you concluded that history has not presented us with a situation of 'final solutions' on the scale known to the world since the horrors of the Holocaust. This book has been regarded as one of your masterpieces, among other reasons because it revealed that the 'Final Solution was not a dysfunction of modern rationality but rather its shocking product'.[1] The Holocaust, you explained, would have been unthinkable without the rationality behind bureaucracy and technology.[2] Twenty years after you published it, this next question asks whether the concept of 'final solution' is of any relevance in the wider international community as we advance well into the twenty-first century. It asks whether we could be entering an era of new manifestations of extermination and ethnic cleansing, in more sophisticated and, admittedly, less brutal and less horrific forms than the ones experienced in the Holocaust.*

In your conversations with Keith Tester, you noted: 'Given the overall weakening of the "undivided sovereignty" of the state, "final solutions" in our part of the world are unlikely to be perpetrated. There is no force able to plan them, administer them and see them through. We might expect more forceful ghettoizations and wall-building . . . rather than new Auschwitzes'.[3] So the idea of systematic extermination was not considered likely in the early days of this century. Before 2001, few anticipated the invasions of Iraq and, later, Afghanistan. After several years' experience of those recent wars, however, this question asks whether it is appropriate to suggest that they show 'symptoms' of 'final solution' types of strategies. Is this a pertinent question? Naturally, many would object that the Iraq and Afghanistan wars do not meet the juridical and legal criteria under international human rights law[4] to even bring the charge of genocide – the international literature and jurisprudence defining 'genocide' being vast, compelling and precise – though, as Schabas points out, the definition and scope of genocide is continually evolving.[5] However, if genocide is considered an aggravated form of crime against humanity (the Polish-Jewish jurist Raphael Lemkin being the first jurist to have coined the term in 1944), and if, as Kuper shows, technological developments have made massacres more feasible,[6] can we draw parallels between the former and the latter, regardless of the fact that your own work is very clear about the uniqueness of the Holocaust? Should we, on the other hand, look elsewhere for other trends and evidence of 'annihilation' plans? Is this a pertinent 'exercise', or do we risk dwelling in paranoia? Can we, for example, identify genocide in the newly emerging manifestations of eugenics and genetic engineering; or perhaps in the effects of the new biofuels industry, which by burning food arguably generates more hunger among the poor; or in the new forms of child slavery and child prostitution; or perhaps in the sterilization of indigenous women or forced displacement from indigenous land across Latin America?[7]

Zygmunt Bauman   I'd say: all similarities are accidental, all comparisons are superficial and thereby misleading . . . You are right, mass murders, time and again reaching genocidal proportions, have not vanished with the defeat of Nazi Germany and the implosion of Russian communism. But then the killing of thousands or hundreds of thousands of people for the sin of belonging to a wrong kind of people, or happening to be present in the wrong place at the wrong time, were not inventions of twentieth-century totalitarianisms either. And they probably will not have come to a close together with that century and its totalitarianisms. Mass murders reaching genocidal proportions have been a rather permanent accompaniment to human history thus far. They have been set in motion by different factors, however, performed different functions and served different purposes.

What set the story of modern totalitarian regimes apart from other gory manifestations of human cruelty to humans was the Grand Design: killing as construction of a new order, and an order meant to last a thousand years, or for eternity. Killing as a way to force social reality to match the elegance of a Grand Design. Something like the statement imputed to Michelangelo in reply to the question as to how he went about producing such beautiful sculptures: simple, I just get a block of marble and cut away all the un-necessary bits . . .

Modernity was born under the sign of a new confidence: we can do it, and (so) we will do it. We can remake the human condition into something better than it has been thus far. Whether by divine creation or a product of blind Nature, the realities with which humans have been saddled are far from perfect and cry out for reform: but to make the world more hospitable to human habitation, its affairs need to be taken under new, human management, with a brief to design and put in place an arrangement that will no longer be a playground of accidents and contingencies but a planned, supervised and monitored order, calling for no further revisions once it has been perfected. The extant stiff and cramping, solid and stolid realities must be (can be, ought to be, will be) melted – in the name of realities yet more solid, immune to haphazard, unplanned, unintended and uncontrolled change, invulnerable to the vagaries of fate. Those extant solids need to be melted because they are not solid enough, not as solid as the realities that human reason and skills can design and conjure up if they are earnestly applied.

I have called that modern stance a 'gardening stance': armed with a vision of perfect harmony, gardeners set certain plants apart as weeds, as uninvited and unwelcome guests, destroyers of harmony, blots on the landscape. The implementation of a design, building the designed order, requires that weeds be uprooted and poisoned, so that useful and/or aesthetically pleasing plants may thrive and bloom, each on its own flowerbed or vegetable bed. In making a garden, the destruction of weeds is an act of creation. It is the uprooting, poisoning or burning of the weeds that transforms the wilderness into order and harmony.

The 'gardening stance' is the distinctive feature of the modern posture and modernizing zeal. What it is potentially capable of when it is stretched over society as a whole (that is, when the totality of the social setting is viewed, approached and treated according to the gardening pattern) has been demonstrated by the attempts at constructing a classless and racially clean society. That potential may be gleaned, though, by studying innumerable modern utopias – blueprints for whatever the writer viewed as the perfect condition in which society would be programmed to remain forever as all countervailing forces were eliminated once and for all and all tremors of dissent were nipped in the bud. Most utopias present only the end product of the Great Design, being rather taciturn when it comes to explaining how the feat of making the design into reality will have been accomplished; the reader will note, however, that the kinds of humans considered to be the 'undesirables' at the time of writing – wastrels, nuisances, trouble-makers – are visible in that end product solely by their absence. Something must have happened to them, mustn't it, to make them disappear during that suppressed, forgotten or rewritten prehistory of the utopia's perfection?

Two fateful departures took place, however, after the demise of the two totalitarianisms that experimented with pushing the sinister potential of the modern gardening approach to its limits. The first was the disrepute into which 'grand designs', sharing in the lot of 'grand meta-narratives', fell. The second was the resentment of solidity as such. The melting of solids goes on unabated, if anything accelerating at a hitherto unprecedented speed, but the reason for that melting is no longer that they are insufficiently solid, but that they are too solid. Melted solids are not to be replaced with solids intended and hoped to be more resistant to time, but with solids designed with greater meltability in mind – easier, quicker and achievable at a lower cost. Ideally, the new solids should be self-degradable, disappearing of their own accord and without a fuss on a specified use-by date, or one to be specified at the earliest convenient opportunity. Jointly, the two departures render the conditions under which a thorough, radical and systematic 'cleansing' enterprise could be undertaken much too volatile and fluid for the designed action to be seen through to the end. The annihilation of a hostile class or an alien race 'as a whole' would hardly be posited as a 'realistic' project. And the urge and stimuli to contemplate such a feat are considerably weakened because the 'final' (ultimate, 'the last and lasting') solutions as such have lost – together with the swaggering self-confidence and overwrought ambitions of early modern time – much or most of their past attraction and energizing power.

There are other developments that cooperate with these two departures to render it unlikely that the 'grand designs', pregnant with genocide, will be contemplated, and make it even less likely that they will be adopted in earnest. The Nazi holocaust, with parts already in full swing and numerous follow-ups contemplated for a later time, bore a striking affinity to the grand design of *Umsiedlung* – resettlement – which, in addition to decimating or completely annihilating certain categories of humans, envisaged the forcible transportation of whole populations away from the territories where history had brought them to settle – both of these in the service of enlarging the *Lebensraum*, the space calculated to be indispensable to sustain the well-being and dominating status of the race sufficiently endowed, resourceful and determined to undertake that effort. The grandiose plan of the Nazis to rearrange the distribution of the planetary population was not their own invention either. It was written into the 'project of modernity' from the start, in an originally invisible ink that grew ever more visible as the modernizing passions grew hotter. The policies of *Lebensraum* came to be widely practised well before the Nazis gave them a name and put an official seal on them.

The times of imperialism and colonialism, and other, though intimately connected, manifestations of the same philosophy of power and domination, are now by and large over. Direct administration of a territory is no longer a necessary (or even preferred) condition of its exploitation; distances are no longer an obstacle in reaching to reserves of productive labour; and the contemporary slimmed down, high-tech and professional armies have no need for conscripts. Wars waged from the sites of 'high development' are therefore no longer aimed at territorial conquest and annexation; their objective is the delivery of a sharp and preferably short shock that will break the resistance of the attacked to their surrender to 'remote control' and 'domination at a distance' by their conquerors. They may perhaps be called globalizing wars, in as much as their casus belli thus far has more often than not been the refusal of the local powers to open their door to free trade and foreign capital, and to offer the human and material resources at their command to foreign exploitation. Whatever the manifest objective,'the latent reason for bombing or invading is the urge to fell another barrier to the planet-wide freedom of profit-making.'

Staying in the assaulted territory for any substantial amount of time is increasingly seen as evidence of failure (in the same way as the aftermaths of the invasions of Afghanistan and Iraq are widely evaluated), not a result of victory. Decimation, not to mention extermination, of the natives to make room for settlers, could not be further from the intention of the invaders (and it is even further from their grasp). Those killed in the process are sincerely classified as 'collateral' (that is unintentional) victims, their death or forced exile publicly regretted and most certainly not counted among spoils of war, their material losses sometimes (though rarely, and only under pressure and reluctantly) compensated. Which does not mean that care is taken to prevent 'collateral' victimization; it only means that, while such killing was not explicitly inscribed in the war plan and marching orders, its likelihood was anticipated but deliberately ignored and dismissed as irrelevant: indeed, as a 'collateral' event, it was neither an event that it was particularly important to prevent, nor one to be particularly bitterly bewailed if it did happen.

We are entitled to speak of some close affinity to genocide in the case of what I am inclined to call neighbourly imperialism – the most notorious examples being the interethnic slaughters of Rwanda, Sudan or Bosnia. They are, so to speak, 'claustrophobic' genocides. Stefan Czarnowski, the great Polish sociologist, was perhaps the first scholar to note, as early as the 1930s, while he was investigating the social, political and psychological consequences of the collapse of the European economy, the intimate link between rising numbers of 'redundant people' (people who could not be accommodated in the narrow range of economic opportunities, nor assigned an acceptable and recognized role in society) and the rise of violence – dispersed and diffuse at first, yet tending to be gradually focused on categorial targets and recycled into simmering intergroup warfare.

As I have pointed out in the past, the genocidal potential of the massive production of 'redundant people' could be, and indeed was, exported into foreign and faraway lands as long as Europe was the sole part of the planet engaged in such production, having pioneered modern order-building and economic progress – the two main branches of the modern 'redundancy industry'. We can say that throughout the imperialist/colonialist era the fast moderniz- ing countries of the globe were seeking, and finding, global solu- tions (or rather global outlets) to their locally produced problems, and the manufactured excess of population was perhaps poten- tially the most catastrophic and socially explosive among the problems crying out for solution. In the course of the globalization of modern forms of life, the possibilities for exporting surpluses of population have dried up, however; in the lands that joined in with the now global effort of compulsive/addictive modernization (and so the massive production of human redundancy) at a later stage, such possibilities never appeared in the first place.

At present, there are no 'empty lands' (more exactly, no lands that can be treated as empty and made empty by decimating their native population) that can be used as dumping sites for the surplus of population laid off in the countries that have recently been drawn into the orbit of 'economic development'. Purely eco- nomic migration, unassisted by army or navy while being severely curtailed by well-fortified borders and strict immigration controls, stands little chance of providing such countries with global solu- tions to their local, though this time not locally but globally pro- duced, problems. The 'strangers inside', or neighbours across the border, are the only realistic targets on which the desperate search for *Lebensraum* can be focused and the only populations who can be subjected to the fate of American Indians or Australian Aborigi- nes. Much less advertised than emigration to European destina- tions, crossing borders to a neighbouring country, often as destitute, impoverished and overcrowded as one's own, falls some- where between the poles of asylum-seeking and violent conquest, and a random accident may decide which direction it will eventu- ally take. All too often it culminates in another civil war, triggering another string of genocidal initiatives.

It is not only 'economic development' that has now reached distant lands that until recently settled for the time-honoured, traditional ways of eking out their livelihoods; nation-building has followed suit, reaching lands given to other forms of social inte- gration. As traditional communities and old communal bonds and solidarities cracked and started to dissipate under globalizing pres- sures, the sites were cleared for new identities and new communal

loyalties. Referring to a wide comparative study, René Girard
advanced a general theory of the essentially violent origins of
loyalty-demanding and loyalty-commanding communities. A
killing that would ordinarily be condemned as a crime if it had
not dissolved into a communally upheld etiological myth, and
been recast as a heroic and self-sacrificial founding act, is the most
common base on which a lasting communal self-identification
tends to be grounded (the memory of such a founding act tends
to be annually revived and refreshed, in the form of a national
festivity, through the ritual of its symbolic restaging). What is
obliquely recalled on such occasions is that communal loyalty and
solidarity is the only protection against the lauded act of community creation being castigated and punished as a crime (as it
could and would indeed be construed in 'alien' renditions). The
original violence transforms all participants and their descendants
into accomplices, and only the survival of the community stands
between them and the defendant's bench.

In many if not all current areas of intense nation-building activity we may observe at close quarters the patterns derived by Girard
from his laborious inquiry into ancient customs and meticulous
scrutiny of etiological myths. Among many differences that set the
violence deployed as the 'founding act' of a nation apart from the
violence characteristic of the Holocaust, and genocidal slaughters,
more generally, one that is especially striking is the emphasis on
the visibility of murders and of murderers' identities (a visibility
that renders the stigma of complicity virtually indelible, and thus
all but guarantees the vested interest of all members in the survival
of community, and therefore also the irreversibility of their commitment to the communal cause). If (as Ian Kershaw points out
in his most recent study)[8] in the case of the Nazi Holocaust the
decision to exterminate the Jews 'was a state secret of a highest
order, not to be talked about even by the initiated' and 'camou-
flage language was used in discussions at the highest level', in the
case of the three-cornered genocidal initiatives in Bosnia, or the
Hutu–Tutsi massacres, close neighbours or workmates were preferred in the role of executioners to make sure that the faces and
names of the murderers wouldn't be forgotten by victims, and that
their personal responsibility for killing the victims would be
forever remembered by their murderers. After all, what renders
the collectively committed crime such an effective instrument of

community-building is precisely the personalization of complicity and the individualization of guilt.

I repeat: mass murders reaching or threatening to reach genocidal proportions arise, it seems, from various social tensions and serve various purposes. Only some of them belong to the class of intended 'final solutions' – wholesale, total, allowing no exception, the extermination of an entire population leaving no witnesses and no survivors, and thus no likely (indeed no possible) avengers. And let me add that none of the intended final solutions managed in practice to become *Endlösungen* – final, 'conclusive': according to the most common estimates, the Nazis managed to annihilate 6 million Jews altogether, while aiming to murder 11 million. And in the case of crimes founding and sustaining community, the finality (in the sense of comprehensiveness) of the original slaughter would be downright counterproductive. To retain their integrative capacity, the offspring/heirs of the original victims need to be very much around, alive, visible and resourceful, suggesting that nothing has become final, that survival or at least security are still in the balance and that the time to lay down arms and lower vigilance has not yet arrived, and in all likelihood will never arrive.

Besides, the strategy most widely deployed and most keenly desired in our liquid modern era is to stave off the possibility of any 'solution' turning 'final': a one-way street, irreversible, forever binding. And the idea of perfection (in the famous definition of Leon Battista Alberti, a state in which no further change is desirable or welcome) that used to guide creative minds and resolute deeds when the project of *Endlösung* was born has now all but stopped inflaming the human imagination. From an alluring prospect and a coveted condition, the state of 'no more change' has turned into a yarn of which nightmares and dystopias are woven.

Conversation V

Population, production and re-production of human waste: from contingency and indeterminacy to the inexorability of biotechnology (beyond Wall Street)

Citlali Rovirosa-Madrazo *Foucault's examination of human sexuality was established with a great degree of acceptance and admiration among social scientists in the last few decades. Building on his analysis concerning human sexuality, however, you argued that the normative regulation of sexuality (essential for modern disciplinary control) had been replaced, in liquid times, by gender deregulation. It is your view that the exploitation of human sexuality for disciplinary purposes remains central in liquid modern societies, but that the mechanism of control and its cultural manifestations have changed – a process you examined in* Liquid Love *and* Identity.[1] *This next question links the issue of sexuality to the all-important and controversial issue of population. It asks whether the concept of population – as perceived by the international community since the first half of the twentieth century – can be understood as a way of exerting disciplinary control in the Foucauldian sense. In other words, is the strategic disciplinary control of the sexual body also a strategic control of the reproductive body? More specifically, is the disciplinary control of sexuality a strategic control of population and social engineering? Have concepts borrowed from scientific narratives (which were themselves borrowed from social constructions), such as the 'selfish gene', 'natural selection' and the 'survival of the fittest',[2] been exported to our contemporary understanding of population?*

We have learnt from your work about the impact of social Darwinism in the Holocaust,[3] and the way in which the scientific findings of Charles Darwin a century earlier were extrapolated and hijacked by Hitler, but this question enquires, did social Darwinism[4] also inexorably mark our approach to population? Can we ignore the historical background in the discursive construction of the concept in question: the case of Julian Huxley, being the first ever director of UNESCO, is extraordinary. Indeed, Julian Huxley greatly influenced the discursive construction of the concept, calling, in his essay 'The crowded world', for the very first time for a 'world population policy'. He had strong views on the 'genetic inferiority of the poor', having written that 'the lowest strata, allegedly less well-endowed genetically, are reproducing relatively too fast . . . Therefore . . . long unemployment should be a ground for sterilization . . .'. In his Man in the Modern World, *Huxley also wrote that 'once the full implications of evolutionary biology are grasped, Eugenics will inevitably become part of the religion of the future, or, of what ever complex of sentiments may in the future take the place of organized religion'.[5] Are these remarkable facts only remote references to a remote past in the history of UN population policy?*

From another angle, what can we learn from the population patterns in modernity since the works of Thomas Malthus? Malthus's notorious An Essay on the Principles of Population *(1798), identifying a geometric relationship between population growth and economic growth (the former outrunning food supplies), was influential throughout the period when the international community first developed its narrative and strategy for population policies in the last century. In fact, the United Nations Population Fund today acknowledges that the debate over how many people the planet can support goes back to the work of Malthus and remains influential today. Furthermore, as you are aware, the debate has reemerged in the light of climate change and the subsequent concerns about water and food security. Thus, in the international community today, global population policies draw on a paradigm that tends to oppose economic growth to population growth. Some, today, have challenged this approach not necessarily in denying or confirming the reality of a geometric relationship between resources and population (an equation that might indeed have radically changed in an age of climate change),[6] but rather by identifying wealth distribution as the major underlying problem. Are we in your view inevitably confronted with the dilemma of population growth and sustainability; are we at a historical crossroad in the Malthusian predictions? Is this the big issue of our young century?*

Now, before you proceed, let me conclude this rather long commentary. Since the major UN international conferences on population (the International Conference on Population and Development in Cairo in 1994, and the World Conference on Women in Beijing in 1995), and other related conventions, declarations, recommendations, mission statements and policy from the late 1960s through to the UN Millennium Declaration, 2000 (with the subsequent mission of the Millennium Development Goals),[7] the grand narratives of the international community have become well established, firmly anchoring themselves as institutional practice across the globe. All UN member states had developed population agencies, population policies and population legislation by the last quarter of the twentieth century, most of them later updated and framed under the thematic umbrella of reproductive health and reproductive rights. However, as you know, this has resulted in unresolved moral and religious controversies among sectors of the Catholic Church and other neoconservative organizations. Leaving those delicate matters aside, an intriguing fact is nevertheless worth mentioning: contraception (as well as abortion) were officially opposed by the Bush administration within the US in the last decade, while reproductive health and fertility control seem to be firmly placed on the agenda of development agencies, such as the International Monetary Fund (IMF)[8] (often accused by critics of forcing developing countries to implement policies in exchange for loans – conditions which entail the adoption of economic policies or 'structural adjustment programs').[9] The relevance of all this being, how will recession and climate change underpin population policies? Is the global financial crisis likely to prompt policies with more aggressive approaches? Is there a risk of returning to open threats of eugenics (prominent leaders in the first part of the twentieth century in the international community, including Julian Huxley mentioned above, were very much moved by recession, war and famine)? Are the above concerns politically and economically strategic issues in the decades to come?

Zymunt Bauman   On the authority of the *Oxford English Dictionary*, no use of the word 'overpopulation' had been recorded until the late nineteenth century – 1870 to be exact. And that despite the fact that just before that century started (in 1798) Thomas Robert Malthus published his *Essay on the Principle of Population as it affects the Future Improvement of Society* – the book which stated bluntly that the growth of population would forever outrun the growth of food supply and that unless human fecundity was constrained there wouldn't be enough food for everyone. Malthus's oeuvre inflamed the imagination of many great minds (for Darwin, by the way, reading Malthus played a decisive role in shaping his explanation of the laws of 'natural selection'), but even such minds tried hard to prove that homo sapiens stands out from other species through devising effective means to exempt its own species, for better or worse, from the rule of those laws of Nature. Destroying Malthusian arguments (in their application to 'us') was a favourite pastime of the most eminent spokesmen for the up and coming, boisterous and self-confident modern spirit.

Indeed, Malthus's 'principles' went against the grain of everything the modern promise stood for: its certainty that every human misery is curable, that in the course of time a solution will be found and applied and that all hitherto unsatisfied human needs will be met, and that science and technology, its practical arm, will sooner or later manage to raise human realities to the level of human potential and so put paid once and for all to the irritating gap between the 'is' and the 'ought'. That century believed (and was sustained in its beliefs by a well-tempered chorus of philosophers and statesmen) that more human happiness might and would be achieved by more human power (primarily productive and military power), and that the might and wealth of nations was measured by the numbers of their workers and soldiers.

As a matter of fact, nothing in the part of the world where Malthus's prophecy was conceived and contested suggested that the presence of more people would lead to fewer goods being available for human survival. On the contrary, labour power and fighting power, the larger the better, seemed to be the principal and most effective cures for the bane of scarcity. There were infinitely vast and fabulously rich lands around the globe spattered with blank spots and barely populated, virtually empty territories waiting for conquest and colonization; but huge, fully manned industrial plants and formidable armies were needed to invade and hold them. Big was beautiful – and profitable. Big populations meant big power. Big power augured big land acquisitions, and bigger power promised bigger land acquisitions. Big land acquisitions meant big wealth, and bigger acquisitions meant bigger wealth. And bigger wealth equalled more happiness. QED.

If the thought that there were too many people around to be fed did occur to people concerned with the state of affairs inside their countries, the answer seemed to them obvious, convincing and credible, even if paradoxical: a therapy for the excess of population was yet more population. Only the most vigorous, and so the most populous nations would develop a muscle strong enough to overwhelm and subdue or push aside the wan, backward and irresolute or decadent and degenerating populations, and only they would be able to flex that muscle to great effect. If the word 'overpopulation' had been on offer at that time, it would have been treated as an oxymoron. There cannot be 'too many of us' – it is the opposite, 'underpopulation', the dearth of a labouring-and-fighting force, with all its sinister and appalling accoutrements (dropping out of the ranks of conquerors, tempting the enemy to cross poorly defended borders, losing the competitive war for commodity and labour markets) that would be a reason to worry. Congestion in the local population could be globally unloaded, and the more so the greater (read: more powerful) the local congestion was. As long as they were numerous, supernumerary and excessive, apparently redundant lives were not wasted: they could be recycled into imperial might, they could serve as the bricks and mortar of the majestic edifice of global empire about to be erected. And so the locally fabricated problems would be globally, and profitably, resolved. At the outbreak of the Boer War a panic struck the British Isles when recruiting offices had to turn down a great number of volunteers because of their miserable physique, which made them unlikely to endure the demands of soldiering life. The panic was well justified: fewer soldiers, smaller empire; smaller empire, larger ranks of impoverished and socially disruptive people only good for mischief, and useless for the effort to magnify the power and prosperity of their native country.

Looking for the 'right size' of the country's population, the focus was not on 'nature' and its laws, but on human tinkering with their impact on the human condition. Human interference with nature could be equally harmful or beneficial; long-sighted or myopic; increasing the survival potential and might of the nation or delivering it a terminal blow. Expressing what by then had virtually become *la pensée unique* (to borrow Pierre Bourdieu's expression) in the metropolis of the worldwide British Empire, one of the speakers at the Trades Union Congress convened in 1883 (a Mr Toyne from Saltburn) noted with grave concern that there was

> a tendency in the rural districts to monopolize the land; to convert small farms into large ones. The small farmsteads were being knocked down, and the land absorbed into large estates. The present land system was driving men off the land into the mines and factories to compete against the artisan in the labour market. The working men of the country wanted relief from this immediately.[10]

Toyne's complaint was by no means news – only the suspected culprit and prospective defendant changed over time in the diagnoses repeated monotonously throughout the turbulent history of the ongoing creative destruction dubbed 'economic progress'. This time, the overcrowding of the labour market was blamed on the ruin and downfall of smallholders prompted by new agricultural technology; a few decades earlier, it was the disintegration of artisan guilds triggered by industrial machinery that used to be pinpointed as the prime cause of misery; a few decades later, the turn would come for the self-same mines and factories in which the victims of agricultural progress sought salvation to be charged as the cause of trouble. And yet in all such cases the way to release the pressure on the life conditions of labourers and to improve their living standards was sought in thinning up the crowds besieging the gates of establishments offering employment. That way seemed the obvious one and was taken to be the only one; it caused no controversy. Towards the end of the nineteenth century, however, another axiom was added to the first: 'thinning out the crowds' required more space (later to be dubbed by Hitler, with his characteristic bluntness, *Lebensraum*), and thank God there were crowds able to ensure that more space could be obtained and kept open. So that Joseph Arch, the legendary leader of the

Agricultural Workers' Union, could testify in 1881 before Her Majesty's Commissioners of Agriculture:

Q. How do you set about ensuring the labourers' getting higher wages?

A. We have reduced the number of labourers in the market very considerably.

Q. How have you reduced the number of labourers in the market?

A. We have emigrated about 700,000 souls, men, women and children, within the last eight or nine years.

Q. How have these 700,000 souls been emigrated; out of which funds?

A. I went over to Canada, and I made arrangements with the Canadian Government to give them so much and we found so much from the funds of the trade.[11]

Another factor prompting the export of internally produced 'social problems' through a massive, and in this case enforced, deportation of the affected part of the population was the fear that the accumulation of the 'redundant' inside the cities would reach the critical point of self-combustion. Sporadic yet repetitive outbursts of urban unrest spurred the authorities into action. After June 1848 the 'mean and rough districts' of Paris were cleansed wholesale of rebellious *miserables*, and the 'great unwashed' (an expression coined by Henry Peter Brougham, the founder of London University) were transported en masse overseas, to Algeria. After the Paris Commune the exercise was repeated, though this time New Caledonia was selected as the destination.[12] *Lebensraum* had many splendours. To enjoy them, though, one needed power. And power needed numbers.

From the very beginning, the modern era was a time of massive migration. So far uncounted and perhaps uncountable masses of people moved around the globe, leaving native countries that offered little hope of livelihood for distant foreign lands promising better fortune. The prevalent trajectories changed over time, depending on the drifting centres and 'hot spots' of modernization, but as a rule the migrants wandered from the 'more developed' (more intensely modernizing) parts of the planet to the 'undeveloped' areas (that is, have not yet been thrown out of the traditional and self-reproducing balance under the impact of modernization). The itineraries were, so to speak, overdetermined by a combination of two factors.

On the one hand, a 'surplus' of population (that is, men and women unable to find gainful employment or maintain their previously earned social status in the country of their origin) was a phenomenon confined by and large to the sites of advanced modernizing processes. On the other, thanks to the same factor of rapid modernization, the countries in which the surplus population was produced enjoyed (even if temporarily) a technological and military superiority over the territories as yet untouched by modernizing processes, which allowed them to view and treat such areas as 'void' (or to make them void in the event that the natives resisted being pushed, or wielded a power of nuisance which the settlers found too irksome for comfort), and so as ready, and craving, for massive settlement. By incomplete and necessarily tentative estimates, about 30–50 million natives of 'premodern' lands on the receiving end of the enterprise of conquest and colonization (about 80 per cent of their total population!) perished in the time between the first arrival and settlement of European soldiers and tradesmen, and the beginning of the twentieth century, when their numbers reached their lowest point.[13] Many were murdered, many others perished from imported diseases, and the rest died out after losing the old ways that for centuries had kept their ancestors alive and failing to patch together an alternative mode of survival. As Charles Darwin summed up the saga of the Europe-led process of 'civilizing the savages', 'Where the European has trod, death seems to pursue the aboriginal'.[14]

Ironically, though not at all unexpectedly, the extermination of Aborigines for the sake of or as an effect of accommodating the surplus population of Europe (that is, priming conquered lands for the role of dumping sites on which to unload the human waste turned out in growing volume by economic progress at home) was defended in the name of the self-same progress that recycled the surplus of Europeans into 'economic migrants'. And so, for instance, Theodore Roosevelt represented the extermination of American Indians as a selfless service to the cause of civilization: 'The settler and pioneer have at bottom had justice on their side: this great continent could not have been kept as nothing but a game preserve for squalid savages.'[15] Whereas General Roca, the commander of one of the most infamous undertakings in Argentine history euphemistically dubbed 'Conquest of the Desert' but boiling down to the 'ethnic cleansing' of the Pampas of its native Indian population, explained to his fellow countrymen that their self-respect obliged them 'to put down as soon as possible, by reason or by force, this handful of savages who destroy our wealth and prevent us from definitely occupying, in the name of law, progress and our own security, the richest and most fertile lands of the Republic'.[16]

Such words now sound incongruous and revolting – not only thanks to the (debatable) 'moral progress' since Theodore Roosevelt's and General Roca's times, but also for the loss of plausibility and feasibility of the actions they recommended. If such statements were indeed repeated in our postcolonial times and on our multicentred planet (itself a highly improbable prospect), what might have passed earlier as a realistic, pragmatically sound and down-to-earth project, standing to reason, would now be cast as a ridiculous and laughable mythology; at best, as one of the hiccups of bygone pre-scientific, primitive, irrational and superstitious ways of solving problems. Today, the production of a redundant population is in full swing, as before, remaining the sole branch of modern industry truly immune to cyclical economic crises and acquiring new impetus instead of falling out of use under the impact of economic progress – but the old fashion of dealing with the accumulating 'human waste' (a fashion deemed 'reasonable' at a time when global solutions could be found to locally produced problems) is purely and simply no longer on.

One paradoxical outcome of globalization in the form it has been taking thus far is that all and any troublesome problems locally produced, including the problem of 'wasted lives', are left to stew, so to speak, in their own juice. In stark opposition to the enormous advance in travel and transportation facilities, these problems can no longer be exported and dumped on distant lands. These new circumstances, and the claustrophobic atmosphere they emanate, go a long way towards explaining and comprehending the current proliferation of 'neighbourly imperialisms', the large number of civil wars that all too often degenerate into the kind of banditry traditionally associated with gang wars, the rebirth of rapacious nationalisms and tribal sentiments, and the multiplying inflammations of genocidal tendencies. They also go a long way towards explaining the recent invention of the 'underclass', and the widespread tendency inside the 'developed' countries to criminalize problems once defined as 'social'. Let me observe that one thing that the incarcerated able-bodied men and women are efficiently prevented from doing is procreating . . .

One point you made, a crucially important point, is particularly worthy of emphasizing again, considering that hypocrisy is especially insidious when it is backed by the vested interests of the countries that raise the alarm; you can expect a hidden agenda whenever the urgency of the measures to be undertaken is passionately advocated. We can expect a different interpretation, and a differential treatment of the question of the 'sustainability' of the same population numbers, depending on who is speaking, and about whom. The jarring opposition between the philosophy of birth control as voiced and practised by the US leadership for domestic use, and by the US-controlled IMF or World Bank for the 'exotic' uses to which you so rightly point, is one of the most spectacular instances of that *deux poids, deux measures* – two weights, two measures – rule. The apparent 'disagreement' between Bush's anti-abortion policy for the US, and IMF propagation of anti-conception practices for Africa reflects the perfect agreement of both with the expectation that the US will remain for the foreseeable future a uniquely 'high entropy' country, while the destiny of Africa is to remain an exporter of the energy to be consumed and burnt there . . .

In *Wasted Lives* I wrote: 'There are always too many of them. "Them" are the fellows of whom there should be fewer – or better still none at all. And there are never enough of us. "Us" are the folks of whom there should be more.' In my view, held now as it was then, 'overpopulation' is an actuarial fiction; a codename for the appearance of numbers of people who, instead of helping the smooth functioning of economy, make the attainment, let alone the rise, of scores by which that proper functioning is measured and evaluated all that more difficult. Those numbers seem to grow uncontrollably, continually adding to expenses yet adding nothing to gains. In a society of producers they are the people whose labour cannot be usefully ('gainfully') deployed since all the goods that existing and prospective demand is able to absorb can be produced, and produced more swiftly, profitably and 'economically', without keeping them in jobs. In a society of consumers, these are 'flawed consumers': people lacking the resources to add to the capacity of the consumer market while creating another kind of demand to which consumer-oriented industry cannot respond and which it cannot profitably 'colonize'. Consumers are the prime assets of a consumer society; flawed consumers are its most irksome and costly liabilities. I have no reason to change the view expressed a few years ago in that book. Neither have I reason to withdraw my endorsement then of the verdict given by Paul and Ann Ehrlich.

Let us note that the places where the 'population bomb' is expected to explode are, on the whole, lands with the lowest density of population. Africa, for instance, has 55 inhabitants per square mile, while there are on average 261 people per square mile living in the whole of Europe, including the Steppes and the permafrost of Russia, 857 in Japan, 1,100 in Netherlands, 1,604 in Taiwan and 14,218 in Hong Kong. As was recently pointed out by the deputy chief editor of *Forbes* magazine: if the whole population of China and India moved to the continental US, the resulting population density wouldn't exceed that of England, Holland or Belgium. And yet few people consider Holland an 'overpopulated' country, while no end of alarms are heard about the overpopulation of Africa, or the whole of Asia except the few 'Pacific Tigers'. The explanation of the paradox volunteered on the latter is that there is little connection between density of settlement and overpopulation; overpopulation is measured by the number of people to be sustained by the resources the country owns and the capacity of the environment to sustain human life. But, as Paul and Ann Ehrlich point out, the Netherlands can support their record-breaking density of population only because so many other lands cannot. In 1984–6, for instance, Holland imported about 4 million tons of cereals, 130,000 tons of oils and 480,000 tons of peas, beans and lentils, all valued (and so paid for) relatively cheaply on the global commodity exchanges, enabling it to produce commodities like milk or edible meat, attracting notoriously high prices, for export.

Rich nations can afford a high density of population because they are 'high entropy' centres – drawing resources, most notably the sources of energy, from the rest of the world, returning in exchange the polluting, often toxic waste of processing (using up, annihilating, destroying) the worldwide supplies of energy. The relatively small population (by planetary standards) of affluent countries accounts for about two-thirds of total energy use. In a lecture with the telling title 'Too many rich people', delivered at the International Conference on Population and Development held in Cairo on 5–13 September 1994, Paul Ehrlich summed up the conclusion of his and Ann Ehrlich's book *The Population Explosion* in the following blunt sentences: the impact of human-ity on Earth's life support system is not just determined by the number of people alive on the planet.[17] It also depends on how those people behave. When this is considered, an entirely different picture emerges: the main population problem is in wealthy coun-tries. There are, in fact, too many rich people.

CRM *Your work represents a landmark in the historical analysis of capitalism. Your theoretical analysis concerning a historical transition from a society of producers to a society of consumers, and (the passage you just described) a transition from an industrial society to a financial society, would appear, however, to leave gender issues and women in a very strange place. Here an over-simplification of the historical process you referred to in order to formulate my next comment: for centuries women were consid-ered the 'main producers' (in the biological sense) of the 'army of producers' (in the economic sense) – of workers, craftsmen, sol-diers, artisans, peasants, etc., which capitalism needed to operate efficiently and to reproduce itself efficiently. In addition to this strategic role in the production/reproduction chain, women entered into the capitalist market relatively recently by providing it with cheap labour – the impact of gendered work and the female labour force having changed drastically in more recent times, particularly in industrialized urban societies.[18]*

  However, it would appear that women's reproductive role is undergoing other dramatic changes: for the first time in history, women's 'reproductive asset' seems to be much less 'required'. In liquid capitalism, women's reproductive role appears to be under-going a major metamorphosis: her reproductive capacity has not only become, to a certain extent, 'irrelevant', but it has turned almost into an 'inconvenience'. Indeed, it could be suggested that women's reproductive function in the economic production chain went in a short historical period from being indispensable, to being a near burden. Guilty of the creation of the surplus population you have described, blamed for spreading herds of millions of dirty, 'mucky children', incriminated for creating armies of poor across the world, the offspring of the unemployed, crowds and 'hordes' of unwanted, lazy, unclean migrants – which you so piercingly described in various books – women's 'new historical assignments' in liquid capitalism seem ambivalent; while at the same time formidable and, allegedly, potentially dangerous experimentation is conducted by genetic engineering on female reproductive organs.[19]

Hence I will suggest to you that women's unstable, incipient and frail place in the production chain might have suffered a further transformation as new industries have positioned themselves in the last decades at the heart of the economy (reproductive technology and the biotechnology industry). Might this represent a historical break in the capitalist mode of production? Could these industries soon be in a position perhaps to aspire to, and even indeed eventually achieve, in a matter of centuries (or perhaps even decades), a displacement of women's reproductive capacity? This is no longer a question for science fiction. This is not Marge Piercy's 'Mattopoisset' dystopia of 1977,[20] nor is it the 'revenge' of Firestones's biological interpretation of Marxism of 1979.[21] Indeed, at the dawn of the century, we can already see that biotechnology and genetic industries have, for the first time since their emergence in the twentieth century, abandoned the margins of society and positioned themselves well into the very centre of Western economies (thus, nearly 25 per cent of Wall Street shares were said to belong to biotechnology companies as of 2002).[22] Increasingly the fears expressed by some feminists that biotechnologies could in time 'replace women's reproductive power'[23] appear justified: already in the 1980s, some authors expressed their concerns[24] about the 'threats posed to women' by these industries.[25] Indeed, during the last decade of 'liquid times', this has become a tangible reality; the scale and variety of experiments is unimaginable. Keeping track of the enormous number of genetic experiments and technological developments could be an impossible and daunting task,[26] yet it is not difficult to see beyond science fiction. It is not difficult, for example, to imagine an industry generating children assembled from, say, uterus-chips imported from Japan, eggs imported from, say, Israel, and sperm imported from, naturally, the US . . .[27]

So, Professor Bauman, if the oversimplified premises above are correct, and if science fiction is no more, the question now will be: if women (the main re-productive force in classic capitalism) are gradually removed from the economic production chain (never having really consolidated their position as producers), and, if they mutate from a reproductive asset into second-class producers and, later, into alienated consumers and, lastly, into self-perpetuating debtors . . . will they, and their existing (or unborn) children, have become the biggest casualties in twenty-first century capitalism? In other words, is Rosa Luxemburg's self-devouring snake plunging its sharp fangs into women's wombs before it finally goes for the head?

ZB In late modern dystopias, from Aldous Huxley's *Brave New World* to Michel Houellebecq's *Possibility of an Island*, 'motherhood' was abolished. In Huxley's picture of a transparent, predictable, comfortable and incessantly pleasurable world, freed once and for all of the bane of contingency, accidents, sudden blows of fate, of the discomfort and embarrassment felt in the face of convoluted and confused challenges without there being an obvious and/or fully satisfactory response – in such a world, mentioning in public one's mother by name (let alone hanging her portrait on the wall or showing her likenesses in a family album!), if at all conceivable, would be the ultimate faux pas, causing the culprit to blush as he was brought acute, unendurable shame. In those worlds, eugenics (never absent from our thinking in modern times – though sometimes, and in certain settings, relegated to the area where one goes, but of which one does not speak) is pushed to the very limit. In those worlds, all accidentality (of which the condition of being born of a mother is full to the brim) is a product of criminal neglect or an unforgivable mistake.

In our world of spare parts, where faulty products are returned to the shop, where all strain and effort is detested and shunned, all pain and suffering viewed as unjustified, unacceptable and crying out for compensation, where all delay in satisfaction (if it ever happens) is condemned as an unforgivable constraint and a case of deprivation and oppression, where any strong passions are sought to be served together with a handy outlet and a tranquillizer, and every experience of eternity supplied with an 'until further notice' clause, where unfamiliar experiences are preferably offered for a trial period and equipped with a 'delete' key, and all risky adventures are banned unless they have been pre-planned, listed in a holiday brochure and covered by holiday insurance – in a world, to cut the long story short, where a happy life tends to be identified with an absence of inconvenience and discomfort, of uncertainty and of any need to cut back on expectations or male compromises – in such a world, motherhood, conception, birth, and all that follows them (such as, for instance, an indefinite marital/parental commitment, a prospect of children being loved and cared for ad infinitum at a price and self-sacrifice impossible to calculate in advance, are not just a narrow fissure in the cocoon that was promised and craved, but a wide hole, impossible to stop up; a hole through which contingency, accident and fate, so deeply resented, might flow into the interior of the fortress that had been laboriously built and lavishly armed in order to keep them outside its walls.

Claude Lévi-Strauss memorably connected the birth of culture to the prohibition of incest. The first act of culture, he suggested, was the division of women into those with whom sexual inter-course is prohibited, and the rest, with whom it is permitted. That attempt to impose on Nature a distinction which Nature itself had failed to make and would not acknowledge was, in his view, the birth-act of culture. We may add that it was also the act that set the tune and determined the strategy followed throughout cul-ture's long history: a history filled with (or, more correctly, consist-ing in) perpetual war waged against irregularity, randomness, underdetermination, underdefinition, ambiguity – against, in short, the abominable and deeply resented messiness of the pre-cultural, that is natural, world. The long string of victorious battles fought in that war have been recorded under the names of 'rationalization', 'progress', and triumphant march of reason. The end of that war was to be the ultimate triumph of order over chaos, regularity over randomness, control over spontaneity, pre-dictability over haphazardness and frustration.

Modern dystopias as a rule expressed the frequently felt, albeit seldom articulated, doubts about the worthiness of such an objec-tive; they tried to peep beyond the finishing line – or rather to surmise a glimpse of the other, still invisible, side of the mountain pass towards which they were climbing. Writers of dystopias attempted to do in their minds what their fellow humans had thus far failed to do in (and to) their world, what they could not yet see, smell or touch: those writers let their imagination travel the remaining, still untrodden stretch of the uphill path. Writers of dystopias struggled to anticipate the unanticipated effects that would become visible to all once the mountain pass was finally negotiated and the last battle was won – and they did not like what their imagination saw. Dystopias were warnings: if you tread along the route you've chosen, and if nothing (including your own second thoughts) stops you, you will be appalled to find yourself in a land jarringly different from the land of your dreams. What made you suffer and so prompted you to plod on will probably, as you wished, disappear. More likely though, it will only vanish from the list of your worries, and that by being elbowed out from it by new horrors, no less if not more horrifying than the old ones, even if horrifying in a different way and for different reasons.

Our contemporary dystopias (including the one sketched out in broad outlines in your question) seem to peer into the other side of the finishing line at the far end of the long journey started by culture with the prohibition of incest (more correctly, with the birth of the concept of 'incest', of a prototypical act that can be done but should not and must not be done). We seem to be closer to that 'other side' now than we have ever been before.

And this for the reason you've spelled out flawlessly in your question. Not only, as we have seen earlier, has sex been freed from its entanglement with procreation, but the development of new 'genetic engineering' technologies may well allow, in a quite near future, the emancipation of procreation from sex. Sex is one of the last bastions of the banes which reason militates against, and which culture, once it had become aware of itself (once it had passed, as Hegel would have said, from an *an sich* to the *für sich* status), had declared to be its mission and ultimate destination to tame or eradicate: the passions, irrational longings, spontaneity, the random play of accidents, ruptures separating results from intentions, limits to control, predictability made obstinately unattainable and uncertainty immune to reduction – in short, paresis or paralysis of norms and rules and the resulting messiness, randomness and contingency of human life. As long as procreation remains dependent on sex, culture's war against nature cannot be brought to its victorious end. And through procreation, all the subhuman filth standing in the way of made-to-order humans (made to order in more than one sense!) will filter in and contaminate the whole of human life. Stubbornly, it will go on setting impassable limits to the rational overhaul of an infuriatingly misconceived, poorly designed world: that product, irredeemably short of perfection, of an admittedly blind Nature, indifferent as it is to human values, predilections, choices and strivings.

In Houellebecq's postmodern dystopia already referred to, 'Supreme Sister' – the neohuman equivalent of the role played by St Paul in the lives of old-style (that is, our style) humans – teaches that conditions of unhappiness (read, of life: courtesy of those postmodern passions and phobias that promoted the long journey to the neohuman nightmare, life had been already rendered indistinguishable from the pursuit of happiness) will persist, must persist 'for so long as women continue to have children'. What she meant was that there will be far too many children as long as children are side-effects, by-products, or (to express it in the currently fashionable vocabulary) 'collateral damage' of the female pursuit of happiness. 'No human problem', the Supreme Sister taught,

> could have found the merest hint of a solution without a drastic reduction in the density of the Earth's population. An exceptional historic opportunity for rational depopulation had been offered at the beginning of the twenty-first century (she went on) both in Europe through the falling birth rate, and in Africa thanks to epidemics and AIDS. Mankind had preferred to waste this chance through the adoption of a policy of mass immigration, and bore complete responsibility for the ethnic and religious wars that ensued, and that constituted the prelude to the First Decrease.[28]

Sex all but vanished from the life of the late-day clones in *The Possibility of an Island*, except in the solitary ruminations of solitary neohumans trying in vain to recapture the emotions of their distant predecessors which, after so many cloned reincarnations, they were no longer able to experience. For neohumans (us, liquid moderns, in the event we manage to reach the state of ultimate perfection), each enclosed in their own mini-fortress behind barbed wire protecting them from savages, sex is irrelevant. Sex was, after all, a primitive, cottage industry vehicle of immortality – obtaining solely 'immortality by proxy', through diagrams of pedigree and an imagined endless string of successors. Here, in the world of neohumans, immortality is reached directly, personally so to speak, to be consumed privately at the consumer's pleasure; here, no one needs a mother or a father to appear in the world, being as it were self-sufficient in matters of infinite duration. Here, in the world of self-cloning, everybody is his or her own mother and father rolled into one, and the mystery that successive Daniels struggle in vain to crack is what all that excitement, noise and hullabaloo once used to be about.

They try to crack that mystery in vain – just as Averroes did, the hero of one of Jorge Luis Borges' remarkable short stories, 'Averroes' Search', when he was trying to understand Aristotle. The great Argentinean writer has said about the origins of that particular story that in it he tried 'to narrate the process of failure', of 'defeat' – like that of a theologian seeking the final proof of God's existence, an alchemist seeking the philosopher's stone, a technology buff seeking a perpetuum mobile or a mathematician seeking the way to square the circle. But then he decided that 'a more poetic case' would be one 'of a man who sets himself a goal that is not forbidden to others, but is to him'. That was the case of Averroes, the great Muslim philosopher, who set out to trans-late Aristotle's *Poetics*, but 'bounded within the circle of Islam, could never know the meaning of the words tragedy and comedy'. Indeed, 'without ever having suspected what theatre is', Averroes would have to fail when trying 'to imagine what a play is'. And so the neohumans of Houellebecq's dystopia would have to fail when they tried to imagine what sex is. At least sex as we, the ancestors of Daniel1, know it.

There are other factors as well. On a previous occasion I sug-gested that as a result of the mutual separation of sex and procre-ation, sex has been freed to be recycled into 'sextainment' – just another pleasurable entertainment among many to choose from, according to the degree of their availability, facility of access and the balance of gains and losses. But once reduced to entertainment pure and simple, how long can sex retain its attraction and seduc-tive power? The probable answer is: not for long . . .

However thoroughly it has been cleansed of the off-putting spectre of long-term, taxing and cramping commitments and other 'strings attached', it still wouldn't score high in the league of plea-sures and entertainments when the criteria mentioned above by which pleasures tend to be chosen in the society of consumers are applied to it (as they mostly, and increasingly, are). Being irredeemably an interhuman event in which both partners are endowed with inalienable subjectivity, sex can come nowhere near the facility and instantaneousness with which other, fully reified and commoditized pleasures can be obtained – just by the simple act of parting with a few banknotes or typing in a credit card's pin. Even when it is insured against unwelcome long-term consequences, sex requires at least a rudimentary negotiation, currying favour with a partner and ingratiating oneself in his or her eyes, earning a modicum of sympathy, arousing in the prospective partner a degree of desire matching one's own. And then, insured or not, sexual intercourse means giving hostages to fate. However intense (and so desirable and coveted) sexual pleasures are, they must be measured against odds that are considerably more overwhelming than those of most other pleasures.

Admitting that women are different from men (while winking to each other understandingly: 'you know what I mean' . . .), the French are reputed to add 'Vive la difference!'. In the notes of the later Daniels you will hardly find such an exclamation. But neither will you find the evidence that the difference has been noted; that there is a difference worth noting, a difference that makes a difference. Scanning their thoughts and deeds you would be hard put to distinguish Daniels from Isabelles . . .

My question to you, dear Citlali: is this not the horizon pursued by many a feminist, deliberately or unwittingly, knowingly or not, by choice or by falling victim to deception, by design or by default? And would they be happy waking up in Houellebecq's dystopia? Isabelle opted out from it well before Daniel embarked on his escape from insipidity and into nothingness . . .

Conversation VI

Secular fundamentalism versus religious fundamentalism: the race of dogmas or the battle for power in the twenty-first century

Citlali Rovirosa-Madrazo *Freud's reflections on God and his concept of fear are a recurrent reference in your publications. Building on his work, you seem to have concluded that, in both the realm of the state and the realm of the church, fear is the engine of history – fear in our age having developed unique features that you have brilliantly examined throughout your research. Should we conclude from the latter that the state in particular is nothing but a 'fear machine'?*

As for religion, may I press on with an all too impertinent personal question: do you consider yourself a religious person?[1] (Would that make you a fearful man?) Or would you perhaps prefer to regard yourself as a mystic, an atheist, or an agnostic, a Gnostic or, indeed, a man of faith? If this is the case, can I, with all due respect, ask: do you invite God to your desk when you sit down to write? Do you invite Him to your dining table? In our troubled twenty-first century, in our painfully concluding decade, would you wish Him to be invited to the 'negotiating table'? And if so, who would be on your guest list? Would you invite Machiavelli, would you bring back the Florentine genius? Would you perhaps sit him next to Anthony Charles Lynton Blair ... the former British prime minister who might have been able to prevent the war in Iraq and did not, the man who, notwithstanding, shortly after he left office, proclaimed himself the ecumenical

leader of interfaith propagation and created a 'Faith Foundation'
(What a nerve!).

Now, *forgive me some further hypothetical and rhetorical delib-*
eration. If Machiavelli were among your guests, perhaps he could
contribute to peace in our era? To him, the church, not religion,
was the enemy. Indeed, for Machiavelli, a certain degree of reli-
gion was desirable as Ernst Cassirer reminds us.[2] *And, as you*
yourself have reminded us throughout your research, the modern
mind was not necessarily atheist. 'War against God,' you have
written, 'the frantic search for proof that "God does not exist",
or "died", was left to the radical margins. What the modern mind
did, however, was to make God irrelevant to human business on
earth.'[3]

But is it not time to make God relevant again? Today, though,
religion is almost synonymous with fundamentalism. In Identity
you said: 'Modern science emerged when a language had been
constructed that allowed whatever was learned about the world
to be narrated in non-teleological terms [. . .] with no reference to
divine intention'. And then you went to explain: 'Such a strategy
led to spectacular triumphs of science and its technological arm'.
But this effect, you seem to regret, 'also had far-reaching, and not
necessarily benign and beneficial, consequences for the modality
of the human-being-in-the-world'. For you, the 'authority of the
sacred' and more generally 'our concerns with eternity and eternal
values, were its first and most prominent casualties.'[4] *Should we,*
I must insist, read this as a desire to bring God back into the
picture?

When you say that ours is the first era ever to be deprived of
the bridges connecting us to eternity,[5] *are you only making a*
sociological and historical statement, or is it perhaps an admission
of some personal longing? And if all the above were the case, how
can God, church and religion be liberated from their hijackers:
religious fundamentalists and secular fundamentalists across the
spectrum? How can religious 'tolerance' become a matter of
simple respect.[6] *Of course, if none of the above applies at a per-*
sonal level, how would you encourage a dialogue between the
extremists and the simple, moderate, humble believers, and mod-
erate atheists, or indeed a dialogue between radical and moderate
Evangelists, Islamists and Jews and many more? Or perhaps
would you say that the interfaith concept, along with multicul-

turalism, is affected by what you regard as the 'politicization of identity', which you seem to suggest is diverting the attention from the most pressing social and historical demands? In short, can one take interfaith initiatives such as those developed by former prime minister Blair seriously? Is his ecumenical project nothing but a cynical attempt to put a 'patent' on faith, a kind of Blair's Faith Ltd? Or should we conclude that, given the promiscuity of the free market, the common perception that all is intimately connected (the war industry, the oil industry, and even the reconstruction industry) is only an illusion, a tragic coincidence? In other words, should we give Mr Blair the benefit of the doubt: as a repentant former prime minister who, like all humans, made some mistakes and who is heartily committed to interfaith dialogue?

Zygmunt Bauman Your highly impressive, thought-provoking and stimulating essay, which you modestly present as but another batch of questions, is made up of many parts. I only hope that you don't expect me to reply to all the ostensible or implied interrogations or pick up all the threads of the convoluted plot . . .

Let me try, however, by starting from the easiest issue, since it has already been extensively discussed – the plight of contemporary states. There is more to the state than being (as you put it) a 'fear machine' – but not much . . . at any rate, not many things unconnected to fear and/or unconditioned by it. If it were not for people fearing, it would be difficult to imagine the need for a state. As people are unlikely to stop fearing, however, at least in the foreseeable future, a long future for the state as such, though not necessarily for any of its successive and eminently changeable avatars and political formulas, seems to be assured.

Rather than speaking of a state as a 'fear machine', I would, however, prefer to speak of it as a 'fear-management, fear-shuffling and fear-recycling plant'. As already intimated in our earlier discussion of state (and, more generally, political) power, states on the whole tend to capitalize on supplies of fear that have already been prefabricated and stored by other, essentially unpolitical forces, without the need for institutionalized politics to actively participate in its production – or, more precisely, with political agencies 'active through their inactivity', 'interfering through their refusal or neglect of interference'. With the evident exception of dictatorial and totalitarian regimes, modern states capitalize primarily on the fears oozing from existential insecurity, endemic, and in its origins unpolitical – aided and abetted as these fears are by countless uncertainties arising from the inherent instability, caprices and vagaries of similarly unpolitical capital and labour markets.

I've written profusely elsewhere (most recently in *Liquid Fear* and *Liquid Times*) about the uncertainty and ambient fear that saturate contemporary life, and about how the maintenance of a steady volume of anxiety and apprehension turns into a major and indispensable factor in the self-reproduction of political and economic institutions, and I would rather not repeat myself here. Let me only recall that the perpetual state of uncertainty continuously excretes a voluminous, indeed insatiable, demand for a force – any kind of force – that can be trusted to know what ordinary people, tormented daily by the nightmarish awareness and suspicion of insecurity, don't and can't know; a force that can accomplish what ordinary folk cursed with the stark inadequacy of the resources at their disposal can only dream of doing; in short, a trustworthy and reliable force on which one can count to see the invisible, resolve the insoluble, and embrace the unembraceable. To measure up to such expectations, the dreamed-of and sought-after force must be in a sense 'superhuman' – that is, free of common and incurable human weaknesses, but also immune to human criticism and resistance. It could be a 'living god', or a ruler not pleading divinity but claiming to be divinely anointed to rule and guide. It could be a charismatic leader announcing a heaven-endorsed mission and a direct telephone line to the Almighty, or presenting himself, like Hitler, as a sleepwalker following the path laid out for him by Providence. Or it might be a collective body, like a church or a party, brandishing a power of attorney signed *in blanco* by the right kind of God or by a History that is always right. There is indeed a choice between quite a few devils and many deep blue seas . . . Whatever the case, all varieties of the dreamed-of superhumanly endowed force carry the hopes that they will salvage the perplexed from their perplexity and the impotent from their impotence: that they will annul the frightening human weaknesses suffered singly or severally by the omnipotence of a God-chosen and God-fearing congregation, nation, class or race . . .

Obviously, religious and political bodies compete for control over the same resources, and domination over the same territory. Like alternative brands on the market, they vie with each other for customers, invoking the better service they can offer to satisfy the same need. Openly brandishing the coercive or violent nature of subjugation is not usually a reasonable option, and so more often than not the reliance of the conquerors on the diffidence or cowardice of the conquered is laboriously covered up. Besides, the terrifying powers of explicit threats wear off relatively quickly. Populations cast in conditions of serfdom will sooner rather than later find ways to effectively resist the invading force, however overwhelming the latter's military superiority, and make the plight of invaders so uncomfortable that a prompt retreat becomes incomparably more attractive in their eyes than the continuation of their misery by clutching on to the invaded, yet obviously not really conquered, land. Religious and political bodies would rather aim at instilling what Roberto Toscano and Ramin Jahanbegloo, taking inspiration from a half-millennium-old essay by Étienne de la Boétie, suggest calling 'voluntary servitude'.[7] La Boétie's suspicion, which Toscano and Jahanbegloo endorse almost five centuries later, was that, in addition to being ascribed to a fear of punishment generated by coercion, the massive surrender of substantive segments of liberty by enslaved populations needs be explained by an inner human propulsion to settle for an order (even an order severely short of freedoms), rather than for a liberty that substitutes contingency and uncertainty for the kind of spiritual peace and comfort which only a power-assisted routine (even an oppressive, constraining routine) can offer.

As the bodies seeking political and religious power operate, so to speak, on the same territory, aim at the same clientele and promise services calculated to satisfy exceedingly similar or downright identical needs, it is no wonder that they tend to exchange their techniques and strategies and to adopt each other's methods and arguments with only minor adjustments: religious fundamentalisms borrow heavily from the toolbox usually believed to be property of politics (perhaps even its defining property), whereas political (and ostensibly secular) fundamentalisms deploy all too often the traditionally religious language of the ultimate confrontation between good and evil – and demonstrate a monotheistic inclination to sniff out, excommunicate and exterminate all and any symptoms, however minute, innocuous and marginal, of heresy, heterodoxy, mere indifference or even of an insufficiently passionate dedication and obedience to the (one and only) true doctrine.

There is now a lot of talk of the 'politicization of religion'. Much too little attention is paid, however, to the parallel tendency of the 'religionization of politics', arguably still more dangerous and often much more gory in its consequences. A conflict of interests calling for negotiation and compromise (the daily bread of politics) is then recycled into an ultimate showdown between good and evil that renders any negotiated agreement inconceivable and from which only one of the antagonists can emerge alive (the liminal horizon of monotheistic religions). The two tendencies, I'd say, are truly inseparable Siamese twins, each inclined in addition to project the inner demons they share on to the other twin . . .

So what is the 'future of an illusion' likely to be, to borrow a phrase from Sigmund Freud? I am inclined to think that whatever the future of that 'illusion', it will be long. Probably as long as the presence of humanity. Freud ascribed 'the illusion' to the permanent and ineradicable traits of human instinctual endowment: roughly speaking, given humans' inborn, 'genetically determined laziness' and their impermeability to 'rational argument', and the potentially destructive potential of equally endemic human drives, human society is inconceivable without coercion. Karl Marx traced the (temporary) inescapability of 'the illusion' to history rather than genetics, and to the historically evolved human condition rather than biological evolution: religion being an 'opium' meant to keep the masses in a stupor, to stifle their dissent and prevent them from rebelling; it would last as long as, but no longer than, the kind of human condition that breeds dissent and incites rebellion. Since the assumptions underlying the verdicts of both great thinkers have been since their inception (in the case of Freud) or thus far (in the case of Marx) inaccessible to empirical tests, I'd rather the jury delayed its return to the courtroom for the duration . . .

Personally, I am inclined to endorse wholeheartedly my learned friend Leszek Kołakowski's interpretation of religion as the manifestation/declaration of human insufficiency. Just as we are prompted to expect by Gödel's theorem already mentioned (that a system cannot be simultaneously consistent and complete; if it is consistent with its own principles, problems arise it cannot tackle; and if it tries to resolve them, it cannot do that without inconsistency with its own founding assumptions), human togetherness creates problems it can't comprehend, or can't tackle, or both. Confronted with such problems, human logic risks floundering and foundering. Unable to twist the irrationalities it has spotted in the world to fit the tough frame of human reason, it cuts them off from the realm of human affairs and transports them into regions acknowledged as inaccessible to human thought and action. This, by the way, is why Kołakowski is so on target when he points out that the learned theologians brought religion more harm than profit when they leaned over backwards to supply the 'logical proof' of God's existence. To serve logic, humans have boffins and certified counsellors. Humans need God for his miracles, not to follow the laws of logic; for his inscrutability and unpredictability, not for transparency and routine; for his ability to turn the course of events upside down (not just the future course, but also the past, 'already done', as Leon Shestov insisted); for his capacity to push aside the order of things, instead of slavishly submitting to it, as humans are pressed to do and most of them do most of the time. In short, humans need an omniscient and omnipotent God to account for, and hopefully to tame and domesticate, all those awesome, apparently numb, dumb and blind forces that human comprehension and potency to act can't reach.

I believe, in short, that the future of (this particular) illusion is intertwined with the future of human uncertainty: collective uncertainty (concerning the security and powers of the human species as a whole cast into, and dependent on, a natural world that it is unable to tame), and individual uncertainty (concerning the security of the person(s) cast into, and dependent on, the habitat composed of humans, made by humans and managed by humans which he, she, or they are unable to tame). Having failed, and continuing to suffer defeats, in its recurrent and continuous efforts to conquer both kinds of uncertainty, humankind will go on reverting to the 'illusion': its loneliness in the universe, the absence of a court of appeal and executive powers are too frightening for most humans to bear. I suppose that God will die together with humanity. Not a moment before.

CRM *Allow me, while I take a breath, to speculate further in the margins of the issues above. Samuel Huntington's celebrated concept of a 'clash of civilizations' had a point. Or did it? Whatever one may think of the ultraconservative credentials of this former adviser to the Pentagon, he seems to have achieved something extraordinary: to place the 'religious question' firmly at the heart of the geopolitical agenda. Though it may be more accurate to say that he placed, if unintentionally, a mirror between what you called the 'Siamese twins' . . . In your view, would recession present us with an opportunity to revise our attitudes to both religious and secular grand narratives? It may be important to note that in recent times some churches have played an important role in rejecting the moral grounds of neoliberalism. Thus, for example, Christianity has been, to different degrees, critical of globalization, both Pope Benedict XVI and the Archbishop of Canterbury, Dr Rowan Williams, having denounced on many occasions the impact today of what you have called 'the supremacy of individualism'.*[8] *But there is a paradox. While all hegemonic religions appear to feel under threat from the homogenizing effect of globalization, they also seem to feel under threat from the disintegrating effect of postmodern relativist narratives: both these extremes have undoubtedly challenged their historical hegemonic position. How, then, can recession present us with an opportunity for a real dialogue with the representatives of these (and other) churches? To rephrase this question, let me refer to your work again: in your exchange with Keith Tester you revealed: 'I must confess to you that I never felt comfortable about the alleged boundary between the religious and the secular and most certainly never believed in the sanctity of that boundary'.*[9] *And you added that 'the so-called "secularization" of the modern era was not much more than the designation of a vocabulary . . . to narrate the human predicament without using the word God. The word could be missing but the narrative has been all along about human insufficiency.' So the crucial point at issue is, if this is all about 'human insufficiency', isn't a dialogue between the infamous twins of the state and the church (and their offspring) both urgent and possible?*

Let me return to the previous issues from another angle. In one of his most recent publications, Umberto Eco, one of the greatest literary geniuses of the twentieth century and a distinguished his-

torian, warns of both the rise of religious obscurantism and fun-
damentalism, and the spread of religious intolerance, while he
expresses respect for 'customary' religious practices.[10] *This he does*
with great erudition and knowledge. But misreading the author
of the The Name of the Rose, *who captured with extraordinary*
imagination and skilful mastery of semiotics the symbolic power
of the saga of religious dogma, could result in a common mistake:
to assume that fundamentalism is a neurosis reserved for religion,
and that secular institutions are somehow immune to this condi-
tion. This next question, which is divided into three parts, focuses
on what seems to be a distinctive legacy of the last decade: a
dogmatic race between secularism and religion. Naturally, the
competition between dogmas is embedded in human history across
civilizations, as you just pointed out, but the rivalry between
secularism and religion has turned sinister in the last few years,
exhibiting more ferocity and fury than before. It may not be an
exaggeration to say that it has literally become a race against time
(perhaps another indication that, as suggested by the title of this
book, we are 'living on borrowed time'). I will put to you that
fundamentalism (secular as well as religious) may be the violent
manifestation of this desperate race: an effect rather than a cause
in today's violent world. I will also suggest that the political and
corporative exploitation of scientific knowledge and technology
may play a role in this process, forcing us to ask the question as
to who rules in science. Thus Eco warns about the pactum sceleris
between the scientists and the media, and exhorts scientists to 'be
suspicious of those who treat them as if they were the source of
life.'[11] *The 'secular front', exploiting and abusing scientific knowl-*
edge and technology and its battle for power to regain ideological
hegemony over a rising religious fundamentalism, can never be
underestimated. The above concerns are justified if one interprets
worrying events in the religious community such as the disman-
tling in 2007 of the Observatory of Castelgandolfo at the Vatican
as signs of a withdrawal from scientific knowledge by the religious
community; or if one sees the proliferation of evangelistic move-
ments, across the board, with bizarre manifestations of the most
primitive and fanatical nature in the US; or if one contemplates,
with horror, the atrocities carried out by fundamentalist suicide
bombers recklessly claiming to act in the name of God. But
somehow 'the balance' is lost when the pathology of obscurantism

is only said to be present in religion, with a 'diagnosis' of this condition reserved for the latter, thereafter prescribing one single treatment for it: 'moral liquidity'. With the proliferation of religious obscurantist organizations (with certain academics at Oxford[11] having taken on the burden of preserving the historical battle against the religious inquisition ... not without leaving a twin legacy of atheist crusaders and atheist dogmatism), humanity, in 'liquid times', seems to have been left at the mercy of the market. In other words, when it is assumed that fundamentalism only occurs in religious communities, the latter's moral doctrine is recklessly dismissed as illegitimate, pathological and unnecessary. The final question here being, is the decline of moral values a result of a weakening and devastating battle between those institutions (church and state) that you have acutely referred to as twins?

ZB   In *The Art of Life*[12] I pointed out that in our society of consumers, with its tacit assumption that self-care, the pursuit of one's own best interests, and happiness are the prime duty and obligation of every human (indeed, the purpose of life), ethical demands (as understood in Levinas's sense of 'being for others') need to justify themselves in terms of the benefit that obedience to them brings to the well-being and self-enhancement of the obedient. Ethical philosophers have tried hard, and still go on trying, to build a bridge connecting the two shores of the river of life: self-interest and care for others. As is their habit, philosophers have struggled to muster and articulate convincing arguments capable, or at least hoped to be capable, of resolving the apparent contradiction and settle the controversy beyond reasonable doubt, once and for all. Philosophers have tried hard to demonstrate that obedience to moral commandments is in the 'self-interest' of the obedient; that the costs of being moral will be repaid with profits; that others will repay those who are kind to them in the same currency; that caring for others and being good to others is, in short, a valuable, perhaps even an indispensable part of a person's self-care. Some arguments have been more ingenious than others, some have been backed with more authority and so have been more persuasive, but all have circled around the quasi-empirical, yet empirically untested assumption that 'if you are good to others, others will be good to you'.

Despite all these efforts, the empirical evidence was hard to come by, however – or, if anything, remained ambiguous. The assumption did not square well with the personal experience of too many people, who have found all too often that it is the people who are selfish, insensitive and cynical who gather all the prizes, while time and again tender-hearted, big-hearted and compassionate people who are ready to sacrifice their peace and comfort for the sake of others find themselves duped, spurned and pitied, or ridiculed for their credulity and unwarranted (since it remains unreciprocated) trust. It has never been too difficult to collect ample proof for the suspicion that most gains tend to go to the self-concerned, while those concerned with the welfare of others are more often than not left to count their losses. Collecting such evidence gets perhaps easier by the day. As Lawrence Grossberg puts it, 'it is increasingly difficult to locate places where it is possible to care about something enough, to have enough faith that it matters, so that one can actually make a commitment to it and invest oneself in it.'[13] Grossberg coins the label 'ironic nihilism': people who adopt this kind of attitude might, if pressed, describe the reasoning behind their motives in the following way:

> I know cheating is wrong and I know I am cheating, but that is the way things are, that is what reality is like. One knows that life, and every choice, is a scam, but the knowledge has become so universally accepted that there are no longer any alternatives. Everyone knows everyone cheats, so everyone cheats, and if I did not, I would in effect suffer for being honest.

Other yet more principal reservations have been voiced against the philosophers' assumption, however. For instance, if you decide to be kind to others because you expect a reward for your kindness, if the hoped-for reward is the motive for your good deeds, if 'being kind and good to others' is a result of calculating your probable gains and losses – then is your way of acting really a manifestation of a moral stance, or rather another case of mercenary, selfish behaviour? And there is a still more profound, truly radical doubt: can goodness be a matter of argument, persuasion, of 'talking over', 'bringing round', deciding that 'it stands to reason'? Is goodness to others an outcome of a rational decision, and can it therefore be prompted by an appeal to reason? Can goodness be taught? Arguments supporting positive as much as negative answers to such questions have been advanced, none however so far commanding uncontested authority. The jury is still out . . .

As far as popular, folk morality is concerned, it is torn between diverse and all too often incompatible messages flowing from sources whose authority is not much more stable or much less volatile than the position in the top twenty of the latest recording, the position of the latest TV hit in the ratings league of the most viewed shows, or that of the latest paperback on the list of bestsellers – or for that matter the position of any other commodity on the league tables of anything, or almost . . . And what daily experience stubbornly reconfirms, day in day out, is the startling unenforceability of any moral principles. We are exposed daily to ever new proofs of endemic corruption in high places (according to recent reports by investigative reporters of the *Guardian*, big companies swindled the Treasury out of many billions of pounds sterling through avoiding taxes by the simple expedient of moving their registered offices to offshore addresses), of billions of dollars of public funds vanishing into private pockets, with pickpockets and shoplifters filling overcrowded prisons while fat-cat sellers of worthless assets and fraudulent old age pensions, or runners of 'pyramid selling' hardly ever find their way to the defendants' benches – though if they do, there are enough lawyers, chartered accountants and tax advisers who, for a proper fee, will promptly pull them out of trouble. It is for the victims of their greed that bankruptcy courts and jails are built, so that they themselves can continue their business . . . As Polly Toynbee noted in the aftermath of the recent 'credit crunch' (*Guardian*, 25 October 2008), 'after being rescued from certain catastrophe, bankers are as full of hubris as ever; and the government is as eager as ever not to interfere . . .' In a mind-boggling reversal of philosophers' moral teachings, all that dishonesty seems to be ultimately grounded in a safe bet on basic human decency and honesty: 'Luckily for reckless capitalism, the poor are willing to work hard in essential jobs that don't pay a living wage, so they need to borrow: they are mostly honest and easily shamed by debt collectors. That's why banks go on lending to them, as most move heaven and earth to repay'.

For a moral being (that is, a being who ate an apple from the Tree of Knowledge of Good and Evil and remembers its taste), the jarring contradiction between the widespread moral sense of right and wrong and the continuous spectacle of moral corruption creates an atmosphere of acute 'cognitive dissonance' (confrontation with two propositions that are impossible to reconcile) – just as the contradiction does between universalistic claims of an ethical demand and the disaggregation and volatility of moral authorities. As psychologists have repeatedly shown, cognitive dissonance generates an anxiety difficult to endure and live with without painful disruption to cohesion of the ego and incapacitating behavioural disturbance. The afflicted person is prompted to cut the knot – however impossible to be untied it should have been if only the contradiction causing dissonance had not been of an aporetic nature. There are two principal ways of cutting the knot, fundamentalism and adiaphorization, and given the acute, indeed inflamed, state of the cognitive dissonance, both are likely to be widely and repeatedly deployed. In your frame, the first way will be particularly closely associated with religious fundamentalism; the second with what you would probably be inclined to call scientific fundamentalism.

The fundamentalist way of escaping the double cognitive dissonance (of the postulated universality of an ethical demand versus the polycentrism and polyvocality of ethical authority, and of a prevailing moral sense versus experiential evidence of its ubiquitous violation) aims at removing an ethical code of choice from competition with other ideational systems; declaring the sources of authority invoked by those alternative systems invalid in matters of morality; moving ethical prescriptions and proscriptions to the realm of revealed knowledge, imparted by powers beyond human reach, and particularly beyond the human capacity to resist or reform. In short, rendering the moral code immune to human interference; something like Basil Bernstein's 'restricted code' pushed to the extreme – not only dismissing the counterarguments already advanced, but banning a priori the very admissibility of argumentation and denying all need of justification besides the (impenetrable, unguessable, beyond human comprehension) will of the lawmaker. In religion, those effects tend to be sought and achieved by moving the sources and the sanctions of authority beyond the realm of human experience (for instance, the voice from a burning bush heard solely by Moses on Mount Sinai, paradise and hell to be seen only by the dead, or the last judgement to be experienced only at the Second Coming, that is at the end of earthly history).

In theory, fundamentalism appeals to faith, unquestionable, unswerving and unshakable faith: dogmatic faith. In social practice, fundamentalism relies on the density of inner communal bonds and frequency of interaction – contrasted with the paucity of external links and reduced communication with the world outside the communal borders: on locking the doors and blocking the windows. It also relies on a bid to embrace and incorporate the totality of life functions and service the totality of life needs. In theory, fundamentalism demands isolation from the market of ideas; in practice, separation from the marketplace of human interactions. It remains to be seen, though, how those demands can be met in the age of the worldwide web, the internet and minicomputers – all those technical novelties having already been intensely deployed in the formation of (let me use this oxymoronic term for lack of a better one) 'virtual fundamentalisms'. Will the new media prove once more to be the messages, and will they reject purposes alien to the messages they are?

Conversation VII

DNA inscription: a new grammatology for a new economy. From *homines mortales*, to DIY 'post-humans' in the advent of genetocracy

Citlali Rovirosa-Madrazo *Allow me then to move into the second part of this crucial issue in order to go back to different types of dogmatisms.*[1] *A case in point is what I would like to call the advent of* genetocracy. *The emerging biotechnology indus- tries,*[2] *which include the genome industry, stem from the most unthinkable places . . . it was a Vietnam veteran who became cred- ited with the most advanced knowledge of genomics and became even more popular than James Watson.*[3] *Regarded by* The Times *as one of the most influential men in the world, Craig Venter's role, in the concluding decade of the twentieth century, in further advancing the deciphering of the genetic code or genome, and his position in some of the most powerful corporations today, is intriguing, to say the least. In his role in the race of dogmas men- tioned above, Venter is attempting to 'revolutionize the concept of humanity' and create 'a new system of values for life', as he told the* Guardian *in 2007.*[4] *Venter's approach makes it compel- ling to ask the question as to whether eugenics remains a threat or, indeed, whether it has became an even bigger threat than it ever was,*[5] *the controversy over the so called Genographic Project and its rejection by several indigenous organizations around the world, including the* United Nations Permanent Forum on Indig- enous Issues, *being a case in point.*[6]

Now, let me divert further and deliberate again: after the old colonial approach to omni dominium *which resulted in the modern notions of geopolitics and sovereignty that you tackled in Part one of this book, and by which 'dominium' was initially restricted (if it stemmed from divine sources) to the terrestrial globe, a new process seems to have started in contemporary times. In the last few decades it has produced new forms of 'mapping': the new cartography, so to speak, of our age – DNA mapping, genome mapping, and even mapping of dark matter and black holes, to mention the more significant ones. And forgive me now for an extended 'working metaphor': one could suggest that in the last decade we seem to have witnessed the completion of a new type of grammatology in the Derridean sense, a new grammatology – to keep in line with the metaphor – that would appear to serve the purpose of supporting new dogmas. I guess what I am trying to suggest is that the magnificent developments regarding DNA inscription seem to have produced grounds for new dictums, new laws without which transhumanity (the new* humanitatem . . . renunciare *of the secular canon?) cannot be conceived. In short, secular fundamentalism would appear to be in a position to feed itself on the 'canonical text' 'in-scripted', so to speak, in DNA, not leaving much space for 'dissent' or refutation. (This speculation is not to be misunderstood: the formidable scientific developments and what they may represent (and their scientific validity) are not in question here; the issues are concerns such as the lack of governance in certain areas of scientific research, its potential extrapolation for policy and market power, 'bio-piracy',[7] and dogmatic purposes.)*

All the above suggests that humans, at the dawn of this century, appear to remain 'trapped' between secular institutions that often steal (and generate) scientific knowledge with a political and economic agenda, and church institutions that seem to hold on to old inquisition privileges. Can we, in short, escape the battle for dogmatic domination? Is there a way out? Is the global financial crisis an opportunity to rethink our relationship with science and our relationship with religion,[8] and, indeed, the relationship among them?[9] More importantly, is it an opportunity for the leaders of the former communities to rethink their roles and responsibilities to humanity? How can common good be achieved in an age in which morality, religion, politics and science have given way to market faith?

Zygmunt Bauman   Craig Venter is indeed a most (the most?) indefatigable warrior of the genomists' army, and his ambition to remake everything into everything else grows with the insertion of every successive chromosome into any successive cell and the elimination of any successive chromosome which that successive insertion has made redundant . . . Offering his 'guide to the future', alongside a few other frontline scientists (see the *Guardian* of 1 January 2009), he claims that the time has arrived to 'convert billions of years (that is, 3.5 bn years of evolution) into decades and change not only conceptually how we view life but life itself'. Philosopher Dan Dennett sounds yet more intoxicated by still more mind-boggling prospects: 'When you no longer need to eat to stay alive, or procreate to have offspring, or locomote to have an adventure-packed life, when the residual instincts for these activities might be simply turned off by genetic tweaking, there may be no constant for human nature left at all.' Steven Pinker, psychologist, celebrates the advent of another, perhaps the ultimate, liberation 'of man and consumer' (who obviously came to replace the French Revolution's 'l'homme et citoyen', man and citizen): 'This past year [2008] saw the introduction of direct-to-consumer genomics.' Presumably, you will now be able to select yourself from a shop-shelf just as you've learned to select brands of chocolate bars or fashion accessories, and most recently (if there was enough money in your pocket) also your children . . . And as (if we are to believe Venter) 'no constant will be left', you may be able, as well, if you are bored with yourself, to dump yourself on the nearest tip and buy another self, one currently more fashionable and so more attractive, and as yet less boring. Genomics and genetic engineering may be viewed as the ultimate dream of homo consumens, as breaking the last border in the modern consumer's career, as the last, crowning stage in a long, tortuous yet in the end victorious struggle to expand consumer freedom . . .

Engineering human affairs is not, of course, the genomists' invention. The aim to engineer human selves (indeed, to create a 'new man') has accompanied the modern form of life from its inception. Summing up more than a century of dispersed but insistent efforts to design a more human-friendly setting, one more akin to human potential and more suited to decent human life, Karl Mannheim concluded in 1929 that planning 'is the

reconstruction of an historically developed society which is regulated more and more perfectly by mankind from a certain central
position'. The social engineer in modern man believed, as Karl
Popper suggested in 1945, that 'in accordance with our aims we
can influence the history of man just as we changed the face of
the earth' (written in 1945, that comparison of changing human
history with changing nature obviously sounded less portentous
and spine-chilling that it does now, even if Popper was emphati-
cally, bitterly unenthusiastic about the way social engineering was
conducted in his time). With the benefit of hindsight, we can sum
up the long series of modern social-engineering experiments in the
following way: the only consistent and effective specimens among
them were also the most inhuman, cruel, atrocious and outrageous,
with the Nazi and the Communist in the top positions, closely
followed by the more recent (and current!) exercises in ethnic
cleansing. As I mentioned briefly before, treating humanity as a
garden crying out for more beauty and harmony inevitably recasts
some humans into weeds. More than in anything else, social engineering has excelled in the extermination of human weeds.

And yet nothing in that gruesome record seems to discredit
social engineering enough to eliminate it once and for all from the
arena of legitimate human dreams. Only a couple of years ago
Francis Fukuyama of 'end of history' fame suggested that the last
century's attempts to create a 'new and improved' human race did
not fail because they were ill-begotten and bound to flounder, but
because adequate means of fulfilling them were not yet available:
education, propaganda, brain-washing were primitive, half-baked,
cottage industry techniques of recycling humans – no match for
the grandiosity of the task. Fukuyama hastened to console his
readers that now, finally, adequate means were fast becoming
available – and we can put the creation of a new human race back
on the agenda, this time with a guarantee of success.

Fukuyama's pretension to the heritage of an essentially sound
even if imperfect tradition was unwarranted: the crucial variable
in his concept of 'new man' has, after all, been radically changed.
What Fukuyama wrote about was a project altogether different
from the social engineering which, in its intention, even if not in
its practice, was a design for a habitat that would be more hospitable to the all-human urge for self-improvement, self-perfection
and self-assertion. Social engineering was to be an operation per-

formed on human society, not its individual members (though the first boiled down in practice, it was intended, to the second). In tune with liquid modern times, Fukuyama follows Peter Drucker in no longer expecting salvation to come from society. For Fukuyama, the hopes of 'salvation' are invested in (to quote Pinker once more) 'a number of new companies' that 'have been launched'; and in their clients, the 'medical consumers'. Now you will have to buy yourself the gene of your choice that will make you (without the detested need for the 'sweat of your brow' or 'labour to bear children'!) enjoy the kind of happiness of your choice. Whatever is left of the old human dreams of a society in which to feel at home and which to enjoy has been recycled into another vast 'virgin land' for capitalist exploitation. This time, the newly discovered/manufactured virgin land looks well-nigh infinitely vast, as there is no 'natural limit' to its expansion. There is no pre-determined level to which the dreams and desires of successive generations of humans cannot be lifted when it comes to tinkering with their own bodies and looks – and the borderline between the 'healthy' and the 'pathological' has already been all but washed away.

Consider, please, just one off-the-cuff example. Do you know what 'eyelash hypotrichosis' stands for? Most women live happily without learning the answer. Not much longer, though . . .

It is not a novelty that the human body is in most cases far from perfect and needs to be tinkered and tampered with to lift or force it up to the desired standards. Cosmetics is one of the oldest arts, and the supply of substances, tools and expedients for practising that art is one of the oldest industries. By interesting coincidence, though, beautification of the body was also one of those human preoccupations in which the appearance of the remedy as a rule preceded awareness of the deficiency that clamoured to be remedied. First came the good news: 'it can be done.' Thereafter came a commandment: 'you must do it!' And then the threat of terrifying consequences for those who might choose to ignore the commandment. The awareness that by applying the remedy on offer you would get rid of an abominable defect dawned on you as you began to struggle to fulfil the commandment; it came together with a fear that failing to struggle bravely enough would bring you shame by unmasking your unforgivable incompetence, ineptitude or sloth.

The affair of eyelash hypotrichosis is just another instalment of that ancient but constantly replayed drama. Eyelashes too short and not dense enough are not a condition to be enjoyed by a woman (as a matter of fact, all eyelashes are too short and not dense enough; however long and dense they may be, they could be longer and bushier – and it would be nice, wouldn't it, if they were.) But few women would make a tragedy out of that deficiency. Even fewer would consider it a disease, let alone an ailment calling for radical therapy, like breast cancer or infertility. One can live with too few eyelashes, an affliction that can anyway be easily mitigated or covered up with a few brushes of mascara. Not so, however, once the powerful pharmaceutical company Allergan (the same company that blessed wrinkle-fearing women with Botox) had announced that faint and slender eyelashes had been diagnosed as the effect of a condition requiring medical intervention; and that, fortunately, an effective cure had been discovered and made available in the form of a lotion called Latisse. Latisse will make hitherto absent eyelashes sprout, and hitherto inconspicuous eyelashes grow longer and more salient; on condition, however, that the lotion is used regularly, day in day out – forever. If you interrupt what should be a continuous therapy, your eyelashes will revert to their previous abominable (and now shameful, considering that you can prevent it, but have failed!) condition.

Catherine Bennett of the *Guardian* observes that many a doctor thinks and feels that 'women in their un-enhanced state offer plenty of scope for improvement' (and let me add, for a continuous income of medics and pharmacists). Indeed, in recent years cosmetic surgery has been one of the fastest growing industries (if plastic surgery, often confused with its 'cosmetic' cousin, is a speciality dedicated to the surgical repair of defects of form or of function, cosmetic surgery is designed to improve cosmetics alone: the apperance of the body, not the body itself, and certainly not its health or fitness).

In 2006, 11 million cosmetic operations were performed in the US alone. A typical advertisement of cosmetic surgery clinics, now a huge and highly lucrative industry, bristles with temptations that few if any women anxious about their appearance could resist:

Whether you feel your breasts are too small and require a *breast enlargement*, or you want to rediscover the body which you had before having your family through *liposuction* or a *tummy tuck*, we can help find the right procedure for you. The effects of ageing can be reversed and features that have bothered you for years can be changed and a new physique can be attained, which could not be achieved even with exercise and a healthy diet.

Temptations are many, the net is cast wide, there is something for every worry, so that almost every woman can find at least one that she would feel was addressed personally to her self-respect and self-pride, pointing an accusing finger at her personally and censuring her for an unduly lukewarm approach to her duty. For the face alone, clinics suggest facelift, cheek implant, nose surgery, ear correction, eye bag removal, chin implants; if the face seems to be OK, there is something that can be done to the breast, such as enlargement, reduction, uplift, nipple correction. Or for the body: liposuction, tummy tuck, buttock implants, calf implants, arm lift, thigh lift, vaginal tightening or 'gynecomastia'. A massive response to such commercials (and the moral pressure they arouse!) is well-nigh guaranteed. A few months before the recent 'credit crunch' in April 2008, William Saletan of NBC noted that aesthetic procedures had been made so safe and lucrative that

> people who would otherwise have devoted their careers to medicine turned instead to cosmetic work. Depending on how you count it, on an annual basis, the cosmetic-surgery industry – subset of the 'luxury healthcare sector' and parent of the 'facial aesthetics market' – is now worth $12 billion to $20 billion a year. Two weeks ago, the *New York Times* reported that last year, among 18 medical specialty fields, the three that attracted med-school seniors with the highest medical-board test scores were the most cosmetically oriented . . .

And so the story goes on repeating itself: an 'unenhanced' female body has been discovered to be a genuine, hitherto unfarmed ('unenhanced' and thus bringing no profits) 'virgin land', a field laying fallow, and for that reason more fertile than other, already exhausted lands and promising much richer returns; a land crying out for a clever, skilful and imaginative gardener to whom it guarantees, at least in the first years of exploitation, easy and profuse profits (though, according to the economic law of diminishing returns, the profits tend to shrink as the investments swell).

No square inch of a woman's body should be viewed as beyond improvement. Life is insecure, a woman's life no less, if not more, than a man's, and that insecurity is potentially capital that wouldn't be left idle by any businessperson worthy of the name. As no amount of Latisse or Botox, however regularly applied, is likely to chase that insecurity away, the likes of Allergan can hope for steady and rising profits and women can be sure of a long series of discoveries that what they believed to be a minor inconvenience is in fact a major menace that they must fight against tooth and nail (with the help of the right kind of lotion or surgery, of course).

Like so many other aspects of human life in our kind of society, the creation of a 'new man' (or woman) has been deregulated, individualized, and subsidiarized to individuals, counterfactually presumed to be the sole legislators, executors and judges allowed inside their individual 'life politics'. It is inside that individually run life politics that the remaking of the self – through dismantling and replacing the ostensible 'constants' of individual nature one after another – has already become a favourite pastime, importunately and obtrusively pushed on by consumer markets and glowingly praised and recommended by their ubiquitous propaganda organs. The snag is, however, that remaking oneself, dumping the discarded identity and constructing a substitute, or the act of 'being born again', remains to this day by and large a DIY job, consuming time and energy (Latisse needs to be rubbed in day in, day out!), often costing a lot of sweat and labour and always saturated with risks. Most of the time it is a chore, and sooner or later it tends to turn into a bore . . .

Well, the main message of the consumer markets, fully and truly their metamessage (the message underpinning and rendering meaningful all other messages), is the indignity of all and any discomfort and inconvenience. Delay of gratification, complexity of a task transcending the skills, tools and/or resources already possessed by its performers, and a combination of the two (the need to engage in long-term training and labour to make the gratification of desire feasible) are condemned a priori as unjustified and unjustifiable, and above all unnecessary and avoidable. It is from the sinking in and absorption of that message that consumer markets draw most of their seductive powers. The multifaceted art of life could, so the message goes, be reduced to just one technique: that of wise and dedicated shopping. The goods and services on offer all focus, ultimately, on getting the practice of life art free from all things and acts that are awkward, cumbersome, time-consuming, inconvenient, uncomfortable, ridden with risk and uncertain of success. It is the effortlessness of the satisfaction of desire and a short-cut to the satisfaction of desire that is sought, and hoped to be found, on the shelves of shops and in commercial catalogues. If the lifelong effort of identity construction and reconstruction is currently a chore and threatens to become a bore, why not replace that infuriatingly convoluted and skill-stretching task with the one-off, instant, undemanding and painless act of buying a gene? As Guy Browning, one of the wittiest *Guardian* columnists, recently summed up, tongue in cheek, the popular reception of the genomologists' feat: 'Soon, you'll be able to view your own DNA on your iPod, and download other people's instead of the tedious and messy business of procreation.'

Whether 'natural' but suppressed, induced or artfully construed, desires are to consumer markets what virgin lands are to farmers: a magnet, a promise of fast expansion and new profuse and comparatively effortlessly obtainable riches. This is, by the way, normal practice for the medical and pharmaceutical industry: once reclassified as pathological, uncommercialized (and thus unprofitable) human conditions turn into territories for prospective (profitable) exploitation. And the occasions for such reclassification crop up whenever R&D departments bump across a new gadget or compound able to provide answers to hitherto unasked questions, the sequence of events conforming to the rule: 'Here is the answer . . . What is the question?'

The promise of the issuers of credit cards, 'take the waiting out of wanting', opened vast expanses of new virgin lands that for two or three decades – until they were exhausted – kept the consumer economy fabulously profitable and the wheels of economic growth (measured by the amount of money changing hands) well lubricated. 'Taking the risk and the effort out of self-creation', thanks to the fast developing 'gene-engineering' industry, may well open new expanses of virgin lands to do the same for the next few decades. Making yourself to the measure of your dreams, being made-to-your-own-order: this is, after all, what you always wanted, only lacking thus far the means of making your dreams come true. Now the means are within reach. Now once more you may take the waiting (and the chore, and the boredom) out of wanting – this time reaching the ultimate frontier of all drives to mastery: mastery of your own being. As Craig Venter juicily and seductively expressed it: 'By inserting a new chromosome into a cell and eliminating the existing chromosome' you can just throw away and lose 'all the characteristics of the original' and replace them with ones that are altogether different and, for once, fully and truly to your taste.

The stage of this particular drama is thoroughly modern. Modernity, let me repeat, was about adjusting the 'is' of the world to the human-made 'ought'. Now, as in its original phase, modernity has invested hope of doing it in the human species: we, the human species, will deploy our collective wisdom to collectively achieve mastery over fate. In its original phase it was the hereditary prince or the people's representatives, with their powers of coercion institutionalized in the state, that stood for the 'human species' capable of accomplishing collectively what humans individually went on trying to do with little prospect of succeeding. In its present phase of the individualized society of consumers, it is consumer markets, vested with powers of seduction, that stand for the 'human species', slipping into the role vacated by the State or the 'Great Society'.

CRM *Pascal has often been summoned up in your work, one of the most notable passages in his* Pensées *being quoted wonderfully to illustrate some of the philosophical and epistemological problems that we are faced with when discussing the Universe and God. Drawing on a celebrated quotation from the French mathematician and theologian, you agreed in one of your texts that: 'the universe escapes all understanding'. But then you went on to state something that a certain Oxford academic might perhaps not look on favourably – in fact, it could infuriate his dogmatic sensibility – 'The Big Bang does not appear more comprehensible than the six-day creation'.*[10]

Now, that was said by you in 2004. Four years later, in September 2008, scientists gathered in Geneva launched an experiment to recreate the conditions in the universe moments after the Big Bang. The Large Hadron Collider, a £3.6 billion device, was to become the experiment by which a 'theory of everything' could be tested. The experiment[11] *also concerns, if I understand it cor-*

rectly, a quest to unify the cornerstone of modern physics, quantum and gravity theory, while it involves identifying and mapping dark matter and the search for black holes. Following these remarkable developments, I find it compelling to invoke Richard P. Feynman: 'Is no one inspired by our present picture of the universe!?'[12] (May I be forgiven for a self-indulgent diversion: black holes evoke objects of desire, bits for a necklace threaded with white pearls; concepts that can only be grasped in the safe confines of a poem, or in daring incursions of a paintbrush dancing over a white canvas . . .) My question to you, now, being: have you changed your views on the matter since the latest developments, or have the most recent Geneva experiments (incidentally not completed due to an 'electrical failure' . . . or was it a leak of tons of liquid helium . . .), has the experiment persuaded you that, after all, everything is (or is about to become) comprehensible? Persuaded or not by the grandeur of these experiments, do you have any concerns about the way in which they are discursively constructed outside the scientific community?

With these undoubtedly magnificent experiments (along with those equally magnificent developments in the field of DNA research and genetic engineering mentioned above), are we crowning a new era of grand scientific narratives. Could the latter exacerbate the dogmatic race mentioned before? Fascinating and scientifically revealing as these experiments are (with allegedly great potential for technology, and indeed further enhancing the existing body of knowledge of physics), could their grand narrative be exploited to extrapolate the moral authority of science into political control? If the former's idea of the Origin of the Universe is finally accepted (with the 'theory of everything') could 'liquid times' be entering their final and decisive stage? In other words, could liquid morality be made 'scientifically justified'? Scientific institutions and scientists, once associated with heroes who challenged the monopoly of truth so jealously held by the Christian Church at the threshold of modernity, appear to be involved in the construction of yet another epistemological monopoly.

Are you worried at all that these extraordinary and unprecedented experiments, consolidating an existing body of knowledge, could be used to condition progress in other areas of knowledge? Would you have concerns that drawing on the authority and legitimacy of, for example nanotechnology[13] (or any other product presumably associated with the 'theory of everything') could become increasingly dominant in policy-making, corporative power, etc.?[14] *Should we, in short, be concerned about the ways in which scientific knowledge can be politically extrapolated and exploited for purposes of domination? – (Of course, there are convenient and alternative metaphors – 'the God particle' for those with religious and spiritual longings.)*[15] *In short, Professor Bauman, the grandiloquence of the 'theory of everything' (like the grandiloquence of genetics and biotechnology constructs) could easily be extrapolated and exploited to complete the dysfunctional body of our societies with the 'invisible hand of the market', an invisible brain of the (increasingly absent) state (with the all-too-convenient invisible eyes of Big Brother), all in order to justify anything from social policies to marketing (. . . why can't they all leave us alone?).*

Let me now move into a wider, but also relevant context: the so-called 'Alan Sokal affair', a dispute over postmodernism and scientific knowledge between Sokal (a scientist from New York University) and some social science academics.[16] *The query to you now being, did all this debate have anything to do with your decision to abandon postmodernism earlier in your work? Let me conclude at last. Is it possible to separate the scientific institutions from the power structures outside the scientific community? Can we approach science by ignoring its links to the corporate world? Have they developed a symbiotic relationship? Has the time come to write about 'liquid science'?*

ZB The term 'theory of everything', coined originally (with an eminently satirical and sarcastic intention) by the great Polish science-fiction writer Stanisław Lem, himself a cosmologist and astronomer of breathtaking erudition, was deployed in 1986 by the physicist John Ellis to denote for the first time a postulated filling of the gap between quantum mechanics, accounting for the physics of objects roughly on a par with human dimensions, and general relativity, used successfully to account for the level of galactics, stars, black holes, etc. If I – a lay admirer but in no way a practitioner of cosmology and all but an ignoramus in its mathematics – get it right: if you introduce the 'fourth force', gravity, to the equations deployed in quantum mechanics, they would give absurdly infinite solutions, which renders the two theories incompatible and unmixable, though both are indispensable in narrating the physics of the universe. Albert Einstein spent the last decades of his life trying in vain to merge the two theories. Since his death more than half a century ago, legions of great scholars have tried to resolve the quandary, also with no results. Again, if I get it right (of which I am anything but sure), the Swiss Hadron Collider was constructed primarily in order to reconstruct the condition of the universe in the first seconds after the 'Big Bang' and so to conclusively confirm or refute the existence of the so-called 'Higgs boson', a hypothetical 'missing particle' without which the evidence thus far possessed of the structure of matter does not 'come together' or collate. Scientists admit that the non-discovery of the Higgs boson would throw them back to their drawing boards, proving that for many years their theoretical debates have been following a wrong route. At the time of these words, the question of the closeness, and indeed the plausibility of a 'theory of everything', in John Ellis's sense, remains wide open.

I freely and frankly admit that the whole 'theory of everything' affair leaves me rather lukewarm. In my sixty years of dabbling in sociology, I have had enough time to get used to a very similar quandary that appeared well before the present one made its way into the focus of public attention; and more than enough time to live and work without its resolution (though, I hurry to admit, that other quandary never became as sexy as the 'theory of everything' affair, since the sums engaged in its resolution were comparable to those swallowed up by the Hadron construction). The quandary I mean was how to tie together 'macro' and 'micro' sociology; it has haunted my discipline since its beginning and seems to be no closer to resolution now than it was at its birth. As in cosmology, so in social science, we are still nowhere near a 'theory of everything', though many schemes that looked attractive on paper yet were of little use in practical work have been proposed at various points and by various schools, only to be rejected or forgotten. In sociology, as in cosmology, many minds are devoted to discovering or inventing a unified theory that will operate equally well at the level of interhuman relationships and at the level of societies (and other 'imagined totalities'), but I do not count my own humble and mediocre mind among them. I am by and large satisfied that in sociology we have developed (and continue to develop) two rather loosely connected conceptual networks, one serving relatively well to narrate what is happening at the level of human encounters (and how, and why) – partnerships, families, neighbourhoods, interpersonal attraction and repulsion, friendship and enmity – and another to narrate what is happening (and how, and why) at the level of the overall social conditions under which all those human relations are tied together or broken apart.

I believe that it is truly important to our understanding to remember and to abide by Durkheim's conclusion, a hundred years old, that society is 'more than a sum of its parts' (that, in other words, attributes and processes emerge at a higher level of a 'social whole' that can't be found in, and should not be imputed to, its ingredients – and vice versa), or Simmel's eye-opening analysis of the profound differences even between the 'dyad' and the 'triad' (twosome and threesome settings), each crying for different questions to be asked and demanding different conceptual sets to answer them. I believe that reducing one level to another, whether upwards or downwards (treating macrosociological phenomena as microsociological ones 'writ large', or microsociological phenomena as unmediated imprints or effects/derivatives of macrosociological ones), will hardly improve our understanding of human life-in-society, while it will play havoc with even the exceedingly modest ability to predict social trends and control them which sociologists have managed to acquire over the years. And I doubt whether, in the event the cosmologists succeed where my fellow sociologists have failed, all those issues you rightly posit concerning the positioning of science in society and its impact on the present and the future of human history will substantially alter.

You and I seem to agree that what truly matters to the human condition is not so much the substantive content of scientific discoveries or constructs, but the uses to which they are put by people other than the scientists (when or if scientists share in the activities of those 'others', they suspend for the duration their strictly science-bound roles) – in our time and place, mostly by politicians and businessmen. One can argue endlessly whether the idea of atomic fission could ever have occurred to scientists and technologists if this or that discovery had not been made by this or that scholar at this or that time, or whether it would have occurred much later than it did – but we know for sure that Einstein's frenetic attempts to prevent the annihilation of Hiroshima and Nagasaki proved unambiguously abortive. The question of the human consequences of scientific discoveries is ultimately a socio-logical question, not a question of physics or any other of the self-proclaimed 'hard' sciences. And the immediate answer that comes to my (sociological) mind has become, since its articulation by Karl Marx, pretty trivial: humans make their history, but not under conditions of their choice.

This is, I admit, a very preliminary answer. By now, science has earned the place (or has been cast in the place) of Rudolf Otto's 'numinous' (the 'numinous' is a mystery – Latin *mysterium*) – that is, both terrifying, *tremendum*, and fascinating, *fascinans*, at the same time) ascribed originally, in Otto's 1917 study, to the idea of God (or more generally to the Sacred – Latin *sacrum*, German *Das Heilige*). This is, admittedly, an intrinsically ambiguous quality, breeding appropriately ambivalent sentiments. Facing science, we experience something akin to what our ancestors felt in the face of a Nature as yet unmediated (and obviously untamed) by human-made artifices: Bakhtin's 'cosmic horror' and over-whelming, irresistible awe, a mixture where proportions vary all along an axis separating and connecting a pole of unmitigated terror and a pole of a devout and sanctimonious, unadulterated admiration and often fanatical adoration. Wherever on that axis the experience of science is plotted, and whatever the stance even-tually taken, seldom if ever are optimist and boisterous sounds completely free of at least residual tinges of a fear caused by the unredeemable mysteriousness of science – caused in its turn by the trivial fact that so many of its findings defy the understanding and imagination of ordinary humans, but also by a much more seminal factor: in the incessant forward march of science, there is always another corner to be turned, another mystery to be cracked, another terrifying possibility to be scrutinized and clarified. Science, that long and perhaps unending march towards the stub-bornly receding horizon of certainty, is a powerful and efficient industry of uncertainties – and uncertainty is the most fertile mother of fears.

As for the 'Sokal affair', it hardly touched what lies at the bottom of the disagreement between the 'fundamentalists of sci-entific truth' and the 'fundamentalists of relativity of truths'. Karl Popper solved that issue for me (that is, proved to my satisfaction at least the unresolvability of that issue), pointing out that the amazing creative potential of science lies in its power of refutation, not in the power of its proofs; the proofs are doomed to remain forever 'career reports', acceptable solely until further notice, on condition that no evidence to the contrary has (thus far, only thus far) been supplied. The greatness of science consists in the fact of its standing invitation to critique and refutation. The history of science is equally a long track of mind-boggling discoveries and inventions, and a graveyard of similarly mind-boggling errors, blunders and false tracks. It is in its modesty and self-criticism, not in its arrogance and self-confidence (or that of its self-appointed prophets), that the tremendous cognitive potential of science is grounded. Scientific truths, as I believe, have the status of forever open hypotheses, never fully free from the risk of invalidation. Scientists worthy of that name would consent that there is not, and cannot be, such a thing as an ultimate proof immune to all further testing; that in the development of scientific knowledge there are no points of no return (if there were, the knowledge in question would be anything but scientific); and that the impulse to self-criticism is a propulsion that is very unlikely ever to be stifled by any number of experimental and argumentative triumphs. An admission of all that makes, in my view, the difference between the scientific and the dogmatic stances.

Conversation VIII

Utopia, love, or the lost generation

Citlali Rovirosa-Madrazo *In* Identity, *you describe love in wonderful terms. Invoking, as you often do, the work of Erich Fromm, you clearly refuse to surrender to the liquidity of contemporary love. Put simply, you state, 'To love means being determined to share and blend two biographies', and you go on to add that 'love is akin to transcendence; it is but another name for creative drive and as such it is fraught with risks; as are all the creative processes, never sure how they are going to end.'*[1] *What will be the role of this creative power in the dark times of the twenty-first-century recession and the moral political breakdown of our era? Is another world possible for our children; has the global financial crisis of 2008 ruined a whole generation or should we leave them at the mercy, and indeed the power, of their own imagination? What is your legacy for future generations?*

Zygmunt Bauman In addition to what you've found in *Identity* (and what has been discussed in more detail in *Liquid Love*, and again in the final fragment of *The Art of Life*), I would like to say a few words about the seminal changes which seem to be happening among the youngest generation in their perception of the phenomenon of love: its meaning, its role, its purpose, its pragmatics. You ask me, after all, what role the 'creative power of love' will play in the approaching dark times; but the answer to such a question will be given by today's youngsters, who in a matter of a few years will take over the roles both of the setters of the tune and the pipers who play it. Judging from contemporary trends among the young, the prospects of love as we used to think of it do not look particularly bright.

The initial, and fundamental, training in the art of loving and being loved is received by all of us in early childhood; all the later practices are transpositions, products of a creative recycling and remoulding of the sediments of that early experience. The first 'Other' a newborn child encounters is Mother. It is from her that the first lessons of loving and being loved arrive, to stay with us for the rest of our lives – whether we know it or not. And these early lessons derived from this intimate love relationship tend to preform the whole network of interhuman relations. So let me start with a brief discussion of the significant shifts that have happened in recent decades in the closeness and intimacy of parents of children.

In the film *Le Diable, Probablement* released by Robert Bresson in 1977, the heroes are several youths clearly at a loss while they desperately seek a purpose in life, their assignment in the world and the meaning of 'being assigned'. No help came from their elders; as a matter of fact, not a single adult appeared on the screen in the 95 minutes needed by the plot to reach its tragic denouement, and not a single sentence referred to their role in the life of the protagonists. Only once was even the existence of adults (obliquely) noticed by the youngsters, fully absorbed as they were in their stubbornly unsuccessful effort to communicate with each other: when the youngsters, tired out by their exploits, felt hungry and so gathered around the fridge, which had been stuffed with food for such an occasion by their otherwise invisible parents. Later years abundantly revealed and confirmed just how prophetic Bresson's vision was. Bresson saw through the consequences of the 'great transformation' he and all his contemporaries were witnessing, though it was noted by only a few of them: the passage from a society of producers – workers and soldiers – to a society of consumers – individuals by decree and addicts of the short term.

For the parents of future workers and soldiers, there was a straightforward and clear-cut role to play: the parental role in the 'solid modern' society of producers/soldiers consisted in instilling the kind of self-discipline that was indispensable for someone who had little choice except to bear and endure the monotonous routine of the workplace or military barracks, and who in their later years was expected to serve their children in turn as a personal role model of normatively regulated behaviour. There was a strong, mutually reinforcing feedback between the demands of the factory floor and military barracks, on the one hand, and a family ruled by principles of supervision and obedience, trust and commitment, on the other.

Michel Foucault viewed the case of infantile sexuality and the 'masturbation panic' of the nineteenth and twentieth centuries as an item in a well-stocked arsenal of weapons deployed in the legitimation and promotion of the strict control and full-time surveillance which parents of that era were expected to exercise over their children.[2] This sort of parental role, he pointed out, demanded constant, attentive, and involved presence; it presupposed perpetual proximity; it proceeded through thorough examination and obtrusive observation; it required an exchange of discourses, through a questioning that extorted admissions, and confidences that went beyond the questions already asked. It implied a physical closeness and sharing of thoughts and emotions.

Foucault suggested that in that perpetual campaign to strengthen the parental role and its disciplining impact 'the child's "vice" was not so much an enemy as a support'; 'wherever there was a chance that [vice] might appear, devices of surveillance were installed; traps were laid for compelling admissions.' Bathrooms and bedrooms were sites of the greatest danger, the most fertile soil for children's morbid sexual inclinations – and so they were the sites calling for particularly close, intimate, unrelenting supervision, and of course for constant parental presence.

In our liquid modern times, the masturbation panic has been replaced by the sexual abuse panic. The hidden menace, the cause of the new panic, does not lurk in the children's, but in their parents' sexuality. Bathrooms and bedrooms are seen, as before, as dens of gruesome vice, but it is now the parents who stand accused of being the sinners. Whether openly declared and manifest, or latent and tacit, the ends of the present war are a slackening of parental control, a renunciation of parents' ubiquitous and obtrusive presence, a setting and maintaining of a distance between the 'old' and the 'young' inside the family and the circle of its friends; in short, the exact opposites of the purposes of the bygone campaigns.

As to the present panic, a recent report by the Institut National de la Démographie shows that in the six years from 2000 to 2006 the number of men and women recalling cases of sexual abuse in their childhood almost tripled (from 2.7 per cent to 7.3 per cent – to 16 per cent of women and 5 per cent of men).[3] The authors of the report underline that 'the rise does not prove the growing incidence of aggression, but a growing inclination to report rape events in scientific surveys, reflecting the lowering of the threshold of tolerance to violence' – but it is tempting to add that it reflects as well a rising, media-insinuated tendency to explain the current psychological problems of adults by a presumed childhood experience of sexual harassment, rather than by childhood sexuality and the Oedipus or Electra complexes. Let it be clear that however many parents, with or without the complicity of other adults, do in fact treat their children as sexual objects, and no matter to what extent they abuse their superior powers to profit from children's weaknesses – and however many of them in the past, in their own childhood, surrendered to their masturbating urges – all of them have been warned that narrowing the distance they are instructed to keep between themselves or other adults and their children may be (will be) interpreted as releasing – overtly, surreptitiously or subconsciously – their endemic urges to sexual abuse.

The prime casualty of the masturbation panic was the autonomy of the young. Starting from their early childhood, would-be adults were to be 'normatively regulated', watched and power-assisted in order to protect them against their own morbid and potentially disastrous (if uncontrolled) instincts and impulses. The prime casualties of the sexual abuse panic are bound to be intergenerational bonds and intimacy. If the masturbation panic cast the adult as a best friend, guardian angel and caring protector of the young, the sexual abuse panic casts the adult as permanently suspect, charged a priori with crimes he or she might intend to commit, or be driven to commit without malice aforethought. The first panic resulted in an increase in parental power, but it also induced adults to acknowledge their responsibility to and for the young and duly perform the duties following from it. The new panic releases adults from their duties by replacing responsibility with the dangers of abuse of power.

The new panic adds a legitimizing gloss to the already advanced process of the commercialization of the parent–children relationship, by mediating it through the consumer market. Consumer markets propose to repress or wipe out whatever rudimentary moral scruples may linger in the hearts of parents after their retreat from being a watchful presence in the family home – through transforming every family feast and every religious or national holiday into an occasion for lavish dream-gifts, and through pandering day by day to the budding one-upmanship of children, engaged as they tend to be in fierce competition with their peers in the display of shop-bought tokens of social distinction.

This, however, may well be a weapon in the parental strategy of 'buying oneself out of troubles', a strategy that seems to create more problems than it manages to resolve. Among those problems, Professor Frank Furedi has noted parents' unwillingness to undertake, and their 'deskilling' in the practice of, the tasks deriving from adult authority: 'If adults are not trusted to be near children,' he asks, 'is it any surprise that at least some of them draw the conclusion that they are really not expected to take responsibility for the well-being of children in their community?'[4] It would be interesting and illuminating to trace the oblique, yet nevertheless close connection between the severely enfeebled intimacy between parents and children (an intimacy that used to be the primary school of the multifaceted-ness and of the many splendours of human companionship, as well as of the emotional and spiritual richness of bodily proximity), and the replacement of an intimacy that was once all-embracing, twenty-four hours a day and seven days a week, with the present-day contacts, instrumentally targeted and perfunctory, and tapered exchanges; with the widely noted peculiarities of contemporary attitudes towards sex and prevailing patterns of contemporary sexual behaviour.

Emily Dubberley, author of *Brief Encounters: The Women's Guide to Casual Sex*, remarks that getting sex is now 'like ordering a pizza . . . Now you can just go online and order genitalia'. Flirting or making passes are no longer willingly offered or considered necessary or desirable; there is no need to work hard for a partner's approval, no need to lean over backwards in order to deserve and earn a partner's consent, to ingratiate oneself in her or his eyes, and to wait a long time, perhaps for ever, for all those efforts to bear fruit . . . That means, though, that gone are all the things that used to make a sexual encounter such an exciting, because uncertain, event, and seeking such an event such a romantic, since risky, adventure full of challenges, surprises and traps – but also of exciting possibilities and glittering prospects. Something has been lost . . . And yet many men, and also many women, are heard to say that what has been gained is worth the sacrifice. What has been gained is convenience, cutting effort to an absolute minimum; speed, shortening the distance between desire and its satisfaction; and insurance against consequences – which, as is the habit of consequences, are seldom fully anticipated and often turn nasty.

One website offering the prospect of quick and safe ('no strings attached') sex and boasting 2.5 million registered members, advertises itself with the slogan 'Meet real sex partners tonight!' Another, with millions of members around the world, profiled mostly to the needs of the globe-trotting part of the gay public, chose another slogan: '*What* you want, *when* you want it' (italics added). There is a message only barely hidden in both slogans: consumption available on the spot, desire coming in a package deal with its gratification, you and only you in charge. That message is sweet and soothing to ears trained by millions of commercials (each one of us is forced or manoeuvred into watching more commercials in under a year than our grandparents could see in their whole lifetime) – commercials that now (unlike in our grandparents' time) promise joy to be instant like coffee or powdered soup ('just pour on hot water'), and degrade and ridicule the distant joys of a kind, demanding patience and a lot of goodwill, long training, cumbersome efforts and many trials, with almost as many errors.

One of the early articulations of the new life philosophy was Margaret Thatcher's memorable complaint against the National Health Service, and her explanation of why she thought a free market for medical services to be better than a 'regularized' health-caring system: 'I want a doctor of my choice, at the time of my choice' (and damn the obligations, timetables, concerns and all the other problems of all the others and therefore not mine, she should have added). Shortly afterwards, the tools – magic wands rather in the shape of a credit card – were invented, to make Thatcher's dream come if not exactly true, then at least plausible and credible; tools that brought the consumerist life philosophy within the reach of everybody who justified the credit companies' attention and benevolence by a promise to add to their profits . . .

Old folk wisdom advises us 'not to count our chickens before they are hatched'. Well, the chickens of the new life strategy of instant joy have now been hatched in great profusion, a whole generation of them, and we have the right to start counting them. One such counting has been performed by psychotherapist Phillip Hodson, and his conclusions present the outcome of the internet phase of the ongoing sexual revolution as a rather mixed blessing. Hodson spotted the paradox of what he calls a 'throwaway, instant gratification culture' (not universal yet, but expanding fast): people may flirt (electronically) with more people in one evening than their parents, not to mention their grandparents, could in their entire lives, but they find out sooner or later that, as with all other addictions, the satisfaction they gain shrinks with every new dose of the drug. Were they to look closely at the evidence supplied by their experience, they would also find out, retrospectively and much to their surprise, that long romance and slow and intricate seduction, now only to be read about in old novels, were not unnecessary, redundant, burdensome and irritating obstacles cluttering the way to the 'thing itself' (as they were made to believe), but important, perhaps even crucial, ingredients of that 'thing': indeed of all things erotic and 'sexy', of their charms and attractions. Greater quantity has been acquired at the cost of quality. Internet-mediated sex is simply not that 'thing itself' that was believed to fascinate and enamour our ancestors in a fashion that inspired them to scribble volumes of poetry and confuse marital bliss with heaven. And what Hodson, in agreement with a multitude of other researchers, found out as well is that rather than facilitating a tying of human bonds and cutting down on the tragedies of unfulfilled dreams, internet-mediated sex results in stripping human partnerships of much of their allure and cuts down on the number of sweet dreams. Bonds tied with the internet's help tend to be weaker and shallower than those laboriously built in real, 'offline' life, and for those reasons they are less (if at all) satisfying and less coveted. More people can now 'have sex' more often, but in parallel with the growth of those numbers there is growth in the numbers of people living alone, suffering from loneliness and from excruciatingly painful feelings of abandonment. These sufferers desperately seek escape from that feeling, and are offered the promise to find it at the next attempt, in yet more online-supplied sex; only to realize that far from satiating their hunger for human company, this particular internet-cooked and internet-served food only makes their deprivation yet more conspicuous, while making them feel yet more humiliated and lonely . . .

And there is one more thing worth pondering when gains are balanced against losses. Online dating agencies (and even more the instant-sex agencies among them) tend to introduce the would-be partners in a one night stand through a catalogue in which the 'available goods' are classified according to their selected features, such as height, ethnic origins, body type, body hair, etc. (the filing methods vary depending on the intended public and on the currently dominant ideas of 'relevance') – so that the users may patch together their chosen partner out of bits and pieces which they believe determine the quality and pleasures of an intercourse (expecting their users to proceed in a similar manner). Somehow, somewhere, in this assembling process the human being disappears: that forest can no longer be seen beyond these trees. Choosing your partner from a catalogue of aspects and applications, the way commodities are picked from the catalogues of online commercial companies, perpetuates and 'authenticates' the myth which the decomposition of humans, animate beings, into a list of inanimate traits originates and insinuates: the myth that each one of us, humans, is not so much a person or personality whose proper, unique and irreplaceable worth resides all in her or his singularity, but a higgledy-piggledy collection of more sellable or less sellable, desirable or useless gadgets.

What happens to sexual relations is only one case of a much wider tendency affecting most, perhaps all types of human interaction. The referents of the main concepts known to frame and map the *Lebenswelt* (the lived and lived-through, the personally experienced world) of the young, are gradually yet steadily transplanted from the offline to the online world. Concepts like 'contacts', 'dates', 'meeting', 'communicating', 'community' or 'friendship' – all referring to interpersonal relations and social bonds – are the most prominent among them. Transplanting them cannot but affect the meaning of the shifted concepts and the behavioural responses they evoke and prompt. One of the foremost effects of the new location of their referents is the perception of current social bonds and commitments as momentary snapshots in an ongoing process of renegotiation, rather than as steady states bound to last indefinitely. (But let me note that even the 'momentary snapshot' idea is not a wholly adequate metaphor: though 'momentary', snapshots may still imply more durability than the electronically mediated bonds and commitments possess. The word 'snapshots' belongs to the vocabulary of photographic prints and photographic paper, capable of accepting only one image – whereas, in the case of electronic ties, effacing and rewriting or overwriting, inconceivable in the case of celluloid negatives and photographic papers, are the most important and eagerly resorted to options; indeed, the capacity for endless effacing and overwriting is the sole truly indelible attribute of electronically-mediated ties.)

For the young, born as they are into an electronics-saturated world, 'keeping in touch' means primarily exchanging emails and messages; an all but effortless activity compared with the time and energy consumed in bygone times when information could not travel separately from the bodies of its carriers and the sophisticated ritual of 'staying in touch', ceremonial visiting and elaborate letter-writing heavily taxed the time schedule, energy and resources of everybody involved. The volume of information produced to circulate on the web now grows exponentially; it has already reached proportions unimaginable to the generation brought up in a world lacking the electronic devices of instant connection (and instant disconnection). Experts estimate that all human language (all words spoken by humans) since the dawn of time would take about 5 exabytes (1 exabyte = 1 bn gigabytes) if stored in the digital form; but already in 2006 email traffic accounted for 6 exabytes. A survey conducted by the technology consultancy IDC and sponsored by the IT firm EDC suggests that the data added annually to the 'digital universe' will reach 988 exabytes by 2010. By that time IDC analysts expect 70 per cent of all the digital information of the world to be produced by 'consumers', that is, 'ordinary internet users', overwhelmingly young, as most of them are below thirty years of age[5] (for instance, 80 per cent of Danish school pupils in the 9th grade are known to send on average five or more messages a day). And let's recall that 45 per cent of survey respondents say that they seek out 'niche communities' online.

Communicating with like minds online is one of the main motives of 'social networking'. As one of the eager community-seekers put it: 'my communities should have similar interests, if not, it will be duck and chicken talk.'

It seems, therefore, that just like the offline world in which they spent the rest of their time, the virtual world in which the young community-seekers immerse themselves in many hours spent online is becoming increasingly a mosaic of criss-crossing diasporas, even if, unlike the offline world, the online diasporas are not territory-bound. Like everything else in the virtual world, the borderlines between 'like minds' are digitally drawn; and like all and any digitally drawn entities, their survival is subject to the intensity of the connection–disconnection game. In the virtual world inhabited by the young, boundaries are drawn and redrawn to set apart those with 'similar interests' from the rest – from those who tend to focus their attention on other objects. The twists and turns of virtual communities tend to follow the meanders of variegated 'interests', shifting and short-lived as a rule, and with intermittently exploding and imploding constituencies. 'Interests' may require different degrees of attention and loyalty, but they need not be mutually exclusive. One can 'belong' simultaneously to a number of virtual 'communities' whose members would not necessarily recognize 'like-mindedness' in each other and would probably dismiss cross-'community' dialogue as 'duck-and-chicken talk'.

In other words, 'belonging' to a virtual community tapers off to intermittent and all too often perfunctory exchanges, rotating around matters of (currently) common interest; other communications, centred on different topics of interest, need other 'niche communities' to be 'meaningfully' (though also intermittently and perfunctorily) conducted.

Paradoxically, the widening of the range of opportunities to promptly find ready-made 'like minds' for every and any interest pursued narrows and impoverishes, instead of augmenting and enriching, the 'social skills' of the seekers after the 'virtual community of minds'. Inside the offline world, duck-and-chicken talk may sometimes prove unavoidable, with the ducks and chickens in question doomed for the duration to roost and forage in the same yard; in the online world, the cumbersome translations, negotiations and compromises may be avoided, however, thanks to the saving grace of the 'delete' key. The necessity to engage in a dialogue, to ponder each other's reasons, to critically scrutinize and revise one's own motives and to search for a modus co-vivendi, may therefore be suspended and postponed – perhaps infinitely.

● Inside the virtual city, problems that haunt the perpetual cohab-itation of strangers in real 'material' cities may be by-passed and for a time escaped: shaken off or put on a back burner. In the virtual universe avoiding 'unlike minds' is easier and can be achieved at a much lower cost than in a flesh-and-blood city, where it will require elaborate techniques of space separation and keeping a distance – such as costly residence permits and entry tickets difficult to obtain to 'gated communities', closed circuit TV, armed guards, an elaborate web of 'interdictory spaces', or other means, all serving to mitigate the multiple threats of tres-passing, 'breaking and entering'. But the facility of avoidance does not bring the problems of urban life suffered daily (whether they are virtual or real) closer to a solution, which may after all be sought and found solely in confronting them point blank; if any-thing, trained avoidance may well make the passage from online to offline all the more traumatic. One can't help recalling Chance (a character played by Peter Sellers in Hal Ashby's film of 1979, *Being There*), who, having emerged into a busy town street from his protracted tête-à-tête with the world-as-seen-on-TV, tries in vain to remove a discomforting bevy of nuns from his vision with the help of his hand-held pilot . . .

So what conclusion can we derive from all that about the poten-tial of love's lights to pierce through the darkness of the times? Having studied the numerous twists and turns of the cultural history of love in the modern era, I've come to believe that, in spite of all attempts to deny it, love can hardly ever arrive in the shape of a 'found object'. Love is a product of long and laborious effort, risky and always in danger of a setback, calling for nothing less than a readiness for awkward compromise and heavy self-sacrifice; that whoever is unprepared to give herself or himself as a hostage to such an infuriatingly uncertain fate would be better to stop deluding themselves that love is within their reach; and that looking for a metaphor that best reflects the typical life itiner-ary of love, one could do worse than choose the image of a fruit tree, that starts to bring its sweetest fruits only after quite a few years of unspectacular growth assisted by a lot of dedicated, intense and sometimes exhausting gardening care.

But you've asked me whether I have a message for those young people still in search of love and unsure whether what they've found is the real thing. It follows from the last paragraph that being an honest person I have no right to pretend that I do. If love is not a 'found object' but a 'product of long and laborious effort', no one can tell me (and I can't tell anybody else!) whether it is what I was after or something else altogether. The sole 'last dream and testament' I may leave is that the chances of bringing the intention and its outcome closer together are likely to increase somewhat once the young give more attention to the condition of the world and of themselves in it. Love is a communion of two unique human beings. But what the lovers expect/hope/desire their love to be is far from unique. It tends to be, among other things, a matter of generation: its shared experience, joys and frustrations, fascinations and phobias, focuses of attention and expanses of indifference . . .

No human being is exactly like another – and this observation applies to young people as much as to old. All the same, one can note that in one category of humans certain features appear more frequently than in another. It is this relative 'condensation' of features that allows us to speak of nations, classes, genders – or generations. When we do, we close our eyes for a time to the multitude of traits that make each member of the 'category' into an 'individual', a being different from all other members, and focus on features more likely to appear in that category than in any other.

It is with this proviso in mind that we talk of all our contemporaries except the oldest among us as belonging to three successive and distinctive generations. The first is the 'boomers' generation: people born between 1946 and 1964, during the postwar 'baby boom', when the soldiers returned from the battlefronts and prisoner-of-war camps and decided that now was the time to plan for the future, to marry and bring children into the world. Still fresh in the heads of the returning soldiers were the prewar years of unemployment, scarcity, austerity, a hand-to-mouth existence and constant threat of destitution; they gladly embraced the offer of employment, suddenly and uncharacteristically abundant, as a gift of good fortune that could be withdrawn at any moment; they worked long and hard, they saved pennies

for a rainy day and to give their children a chance of a trouble-free
life they themselves never had. Their children, 'generation X', now
aged between twenty-eight and forty-five, were born into a different world which their parents' long working hours and parsimony
had helped to bring about. They adopted their parental life philosophy and strategy, though they did so rather reluctantly, and
were increasingly impatient, as the world around them grew richer
and life prospects more secure, to see and enjoy the rewards of
their temperance and self-denial; this is why it has sometimes been
dubbed, bitingly, a 'me generation'. . . And then 'generation Y'
arrived, now aged between eleven and twenty-eight. As numerous
observers and researchers agree, they are sharply different from
their parents and grandparents. They were born into a world
which their parents did not know in their youth, which they would
have found difficult, if not downright impossible, to imagine then,
and which they welcomed with a mixture of bafflement and dis-
trust when it arrived. A world of abundant employment, seem-
ingly infinite choices, plentiful opportunities to be enjoyed, each
more alluring than the other, and pleasures to be tasted, each more
seductive than the other.

Well, without air to breathe you wouldn't survive more than a
minute or two; but were you asked to make a list of things you
consider to be your foremost 'life necessities', air would hardly
crop up – and in the unlikely event it did, it would be far down
the list. You just assume, without thinking, that air is there and
that you need do next to nothing to ingest as much of it as your
lungs require. Until a few months ago, work (in our part of the
world at least) was in this respect like air: always available whenever you needed it; and if it happened to be lacking for a moment
(like fresh air in a crowded room), a little effort (like opening a
window) would suffice to bring things back to normal. However
amazing this may seem to members of the 'boomer' or even the
'X' generations, it is no wonder that 'work' falls close to the
bottom of the lists of items indispensable to the good life that,
according to the latest research, members of 'generation Y' tend
to compose. If pressed to justify this neglect, they would answer
along these lines: 'Work? It is, alas, unavoidable (again, like air)
to stay alive. But it won't make life worth living – rather the
opposite: it may make it dreary and unappetizing. It may prove
to be a chore and a bore – nothing interesting happening, nothing

to catch your imagination, nothing to stimulate your senses. If the kind of work gives you little pleasure, at any rate it should not stand in the way of things that truly matter!' What are they, the things that truly matter? A lot of free time outside office, shop or factory, time off whenever something more interesting crops up somewhere else, travelling, being in places and among friends of your choice – all those things that occur outside the workplace. Life is elsewhere! Whatever life-project members of generation Y may entertain and cherish, it is unlikely to be wrapped around employment – let alone an employment from here to eternity. The last thing they would appreciate in work would be its stability . . .

Research shows that in looking for young talent, the most reputable recruiting agencies are fully aware of generation's Y's priorities and phobias and are at pain to focus their seductive offers on the freedoms the employment offered will guarantee: flexible working hours, working from home, sabbaticals, long leaves with the job retained for the duration – and entertaining/relaxing opportunities inside the workplace. The agencies have accepted by now that if the newcomers find the work uninteresting, they will simply quit. Once the prospect of unemployment, that cruel, inhuman, but most effective guardian of workforce stability, stops being frightening, there is little else to stop them quitting.

Well, if this is the kind of life philosophy and life strategy that used to distinguish generation Y from its predecessors, our young people are due for a rude awakening. The most prosperous countries of Europe expect mass unemployment to return from oblivion and from its allegedly permanent exile. If the dark premonitions materialize, the infinite choice and freedom of movement and change which the contemporary young have come to view (or, rather, were born to see) as part of nature is about to disappear – together with the ostensibly unlimited credit they hoped would sustain them in the event of (temporary and brief) adversity, and would see them through any (temporary and brief) lack of an immediate and satisfactory solution to their trouble. To the members of generation Y, this may come as a shock. Unlike the boomer generation, they have no old memories, half-forgotten skills and the long unused tricks to fall back on. A world of harsh, unnegotiable realities, of scarcity and enforced austerity, of times of trouble in which 'quitting' is no solution is for a great many of them a totally foreign country; a country they have never visited or, if they have done they never seriously considered settling in, a country so mysterious that it would require a long and hard and not at all pleasant apprenticeship to accommodate.

It remains to be seen in what shape generation Y will emerge from this test . . .

Notes

Introduction

1 On the definition of the *ethnocratic state* in Latin America, see R. Stavenhagen, *Derechos indigenas y derechos humanos en America Latina*, IIDH/El Colegio de México, Mexico City, 1988. See also R. Stavenhagen, 'Comunidades etnicas en estados modernos', *America Indigena*, vol. 49, no. 1 (1989): 11–34; R. Stavenhagen and D. Iturralde (eds), *Entre la ley y la costumbre. El derecho consuetudinario indigena en America Latina*, Mexico: Instituto Indigenista Interamericano and Instituto Interamericano de Derechos Humanos, Mexico City, 1990; R. Stavenhagen, *La situación de los derechos de los pueblos indígenas en América Latina*, Comisión Interamericana de Derechos Humanos – Organización de Estados Americanos, 1992.

2 For the full text of the G20 declaration, see http://news.bbc.co.uk/go/pr/fr/-/1/hi/business/7731741.stm (BBC, 15 Nov. 2008). See also http://news.bbc.co.uk/go/pr/fr/-/1/hi/business/7728649.stm (BBC, 14 Nov. 2008). It is important to observe that, following the 2009 G20 summit in April 2009, Prime Minister Gordon Brown declared that 'the Washington Consensus is over' (http://news.sky.com/skynews/Home/Politics/Prime-Minister-Gordon-Brown-G20-Will-Pump-One-Trillion-Dollars-Into-World-Economy/Article/200904115254629). Regarding the controversies around the so-called 'Washington Consensus', see Dani Rodrik, 'Goodbye Washington Consensus, hello Washington confusion? A review of the World's Bank economic growth in the 1990's: learning from a

decade of reforms', *Journal of Economic Literature*, vol. 44 (Dec. 2006): 973–87.
3   BBC, 12 Feb. 2009.
4   BBC, 26 Feb. 2009.
5   See D. Hirsch, *Ending Child Poverty in a Changing World*, Joseph Rowntree Foundation, York, 2009; see also BBC, 18 Feb. 2009.
6   By the summer of 2009 the UN's Food and Agriculture Organization (FAO) stated that world hunger had hit 1 billion, making the figure a record high. FAO warned that 'the silent hunger crisis – affecting one sixth of all of humanity – posed a serious risk for world peace and security'. In a report published in June 2009, the FAO Director-General Jacques Diouf said that 'The most recent increase in hunger is not the consequence of poor global harvests but is caused by the world economic crisis.' In his view, the alarming figure was the result of 'a dangerous mix of the global economic slowdown combined with stubbornly high food prices'. See www.fao.org/news/story/en/item/20568/icode/; and http://news.bbc.co.uk/go/pr/fr/-/1/hi/world/europe/8109698.stm. See also *La Jornada*, 28 Jan. 2009.
7   An example of this can be found in the writings of J. D. Sachs, United Nations poverty programme adviser, who suggested that 'it is more precise to say that exploitation is the result of poverty instead of its cause', see J. D. Sachs, 'Can extreme poverty be eliminated?', *Scientific American* (Sept. 2005): 60.
8   It was not long after President Barack Obama took office that it was revealed that the recession had come to be regarded as an issue of 'national security'. In the early days of February 2009, only five months after the Wall Street crash, Dennis C. Blair, the new Director of National Intelligence in the US, declared in his first report to the Senate that 'the primary preoccupation' of security for the US was the 'geopolitical implications' of the global financial crisis. He also claimed that 'the crisis could undermine the promotion of the free market'. While the focus in his address to the US Congress was the threat posed by poverty in developing countries, for the first time in decades it transpired, according to *La Jornada*'s US correspondents, that 'the main menace to the USA's security did not come from an external enemy – as in the time of communism or as with the rise of international terrorism – instead it came from within the USA' (*La Jornada*, 13 Feb. 2009).
9   Z. Bauman, *Europe: An Unfinished Adventure*, Polity, Cambridge, 2004; Z. Bauman, *Liquid Times: Living in an Age of Uncertainty*, Polity, Cambridge, 2007; Z. Bauman, *Conversations with Keith Tester*, Polity, Cambridge, 2001; Z. Bauman, *Postmodern Ethics*,

Blackwell, Oxford, 1993; Z. Bauman, 'Modernity and the state', *Times Literary Supplement*, no. 4895 (1997): 4–5; Z. Bauman, *The Absence of Society*, Social Evils series, Joseph Rowntree Foundation, York, 2008.

10   Z. Bauman, 'Totalitarianism as a historical phenomenon', *Times Literary Supplement*, no. 4567 (1990): 1095; Z. Bauman, 'Twenty years after: crisis of Soviet type systems', *Problems of Communism*, vol. 20, no. 6 (1971): 45–53; Z. Bauman, 'Social dissent in East European political systems', *Archives Européennes de Sociologie*, vol. 12, no. 1 (1971): 25–51.

11   Z. Bauman, *Modernity and Holocaust*, Polity, Cambridge, 1989; Z. Bauman, 'Is another holocaust possible?', *Revista de Occidente*, no. 176 (1996): 112–29.

12   Regarding Eurocentrism, see C. Rovirosa-Madrazo, 'Indigenous rights, ethnocentrism and the crisis of the nation-state: paradigmatic considerations for human rights. Zapatista rebellion in Mexico and ethnic conflict in Nicaragua', Ph.D. thesis, University of Essex, 1995; C. Rovirosa-Madrazo, 'Analfabetismens censur', in N. Barfoeod (ed.), *Magtens Tavse Tjener. Om censur og ytringsfrihed. Et debatskrift med essays der spaender fra Vaclav Havel til Salman Rushdi*, Spektrum, Copenhagen, 1991; E. Dussel, 'A new age in the history of philosophy: the world dialogue between philosophical traditions', *Philosophy and Social Criticism*, vol. 35 (2009): 499–516; A. Quijano, 'Coloniality of power, Eurocentrism and social classification', in M. Morana, E. Dussel and C. Jauregui (eds), *Coloniality at Large: Latin America and the Postcolonial Debate*, Duke University Press, Durham, 2008, pp. 181–224. C. Rovirosa-Madrazo, 'Ethnocentrism as logocentrism', working paper, Department of Sociology, University of Essex (Oct. 1992); E. Lander, 'Eurocentrism, modern knowledges, and the "natural" order of global capital', *Nepantla: Views from the South*, vol. 1, no. 3.2 (2002): 245–68; W. Mignolo, 'The geopolitics of knowledge and the colonial difference', in Morana, Dussel and Jauregui, *Coloniality at Large*, pp. 225–8; W. Mignolo, *Historias locales/diseños globales. Colonialidad, conocimientos subalternos y pensamiento fronterizo*, Akal, Madrid, 2003; E. Dussel, 'Europa, modernidad y eurocentrismo', in E. Lander (ed.), *La colonialidad del saber: eurocentrismo y ciencias sociales. Perspectivas Latinoamericanas*, CLACSO, Buenos Aires, 2000; E. Lander, 'Eurocentrism and colonialism in Latin American social thought', *Nepantla: Views from the South*, vol. 1, no. 3 (2000): 519–32.

13   Z. Bauman, *Legislators and Interpreters: On Modernity, Postmodernity and Intellectuals*, Polity, Cambridge, 1987, and Z.

Bauman, 'Social issues of law and order', *British Journal of Criminology*, vol. 40, no. 2 (2000): 205–21.

14 Z. Bauman, *Culture as Praxis*, Routledge and Kegan Paul, London, 1973, and Z. Bauman, 'Liquid arts', *Theory, Culture & Society*, vol. 24, no. 1 (2007): 117–26.

15 A. Elliot (ed.), *The Contemporary Bauman*, Routledge, London, 2007.

16 Bauman, *Postmodern Ethics*; Z. Bauman, *Does Ethics Have a Chance in a World of Consumers?* Harvard University Press, Cambridge, 2008.

17 Z. Bauman, *Postmodernity and its Discontents*, Polity, Cambridge, 1997.

18 Z. Bauman, *In Search of Politics*, Stanford University Press, Stanford, 1999.

19 Z. Bauman, *Liquid Modernity*, Polity, Cambridge, 2000.

20 Z. Bauman, *Globalization: The Human Consequences*, Polity, Cambridge, 1998.

21 Bauman, *The Absence of Society*, p. 3.

22 See p. 119.

23 L. Ray, 'Postmodernity to liquid modernity', in Elliot, *The Contemporary Bauman*, p. 68.

24 Bauman, *Liquid Times*, p. 65.

25 Bauman, *Postmodernity and its Discontents*, p. 44.

26 Z. Bauman, *Consuming Life*, Polity, Cambridge, 2007.

27 Z. Bauman, *Identity: Conversation with Benedetto Vecchi*, Polity, Cambridge, 2004, pp. 15–28.

28 Bauman, *Postmodernity and its Discontents*, pp. 35–45.

29 Bauman, *Identity*, p. 83; Z. Bauman, *Liquid Love*, Polity, Cambridge, 2003.

30 A. Branaman, 'Gender and sexualities in liquid modernity', in Elliot, *The Contemporary Bauman*, pp. 117–35.

31 I. Semo, 'La sociologia de Z Bauman', *La Jornada*, 26 Jan. 2008.

32 Bauman, *Conversations*, p. 142.

33 Ibid.

34 Z. Bauman, *Liquid Fear*, Polity, Cambridge, 2006.

35 Z. Bauman, *Miedo líquido. La sociedad contemporánea y sus temores*, Paidos, Barcelona, 2007.

36 Semo, 'La sociologia de Z Bauman'.

37 J. F. Lyotard, *The Postmodern Condition: A Report on Knowledge*, Manchester University Press, Manchester, 1989.

38 Particularly J. Derrida, *De la gramatologia*, Siglo Veintiuno Editores, Mexico City, 1971; J. Derrida, *Posiciones*, Pretextos,

Valencia, 1977; J. Derrida, *The Other Reading: Reflections on Today's Europe*, Indiana University Press, Indianapolis, 1992.

39 Bauman, *Postmodern Ethics*.

40 C. Douzinas, R. Warrington and S. McVeigh, *Postmodern Jurisprudence: The Law of the Text in the Text of Law*, Routledge, London, 1991; P. Goodrich, *Reading the Law: A Critical Introduction to Legal Method and Techniques*, Blackwell, Oxford, 1986.

41 See N. Luhmann, 'The third question: the creative ideas of paradoxes in law and legal history', *Journal of Law and Society*, vol. 15, no. 2 (1988): 153–60, though Luhmann is considered an advocate of so-called 'grand theories' . . .

42 See Z. Bauman, *Socialism: The Active Utopia*, Allen & Unwin, London, 1976.

43 Z. Bauman, 'Utopia with no topos', *History of the Human Sciences*, vol. 16, no. 1 (2003): 11–25; Bauman, *Does Ethics Have a Chance?*

44 M. H. Jacobsen, 'Solid modernity, liquid utopia – liquid modernity, solid utopia: ubiquitous utopianism as a trademark of the work of Bauman', in Elliot, *The Contemporary Bauman*, pp. 217–40.

45 Bauman, *Socialism*, pp. 12–17.

46 For a comprehensive analysis of the work of Levinas, see S. Critchley and R. Bernasconi (eds), *The Cambridge Companion to Levinas*, Cambridge University Press, Cambridge, 2002.

47 Bauman, *Does Ethics Have a Chance?*; Z. Bauman, 'The world inhospitable to Levinas', *Philosophy Today*, vol. 43, no. 2 (1999): 151–67.

48 Bauman, *Does Ethics Have a Chance?*, p. 35.

49 Bauman, *Communities*, p. 140.

50 Semo, 'La sociologia de Z Bauman'.

51 Bauman, *Postmodern Ethics*, p. 32.

52 Ibid.

53 Z. Bauman, 'The demons of an open society', *Sociologicky Casopis/ Czech Sociological Review*, vol. 41, no. 4 (2005); Z. Bauman, 'Observations on modernity', *Journal of the Royal Anthropological Institute*, vol. 6, no. 3 (2000): 554; Bauman, *Liquid Modernity*.

54 See B. A. Bolivar, *El estructuralismo. De Levi-Strauss a Derrida*, Cincel, Madrid, 1985.

55 See p. 155.

56 Quoted in R. Kilminster and I. Varcoe, *Culture, Modernity and Revolution: Essays in Honour of Zygmunt Bauman*, Routledge, London, 1995, p. 41.

57 See D. L. Hull and M. Ruse, *The Cambridge Companion to the Philosophy of Biology*, Cambridge University Press, Cambridge, 2008; see also S. Rose, L. J. Kamin and R. C. Lewontin, *Biology,*

Ideology and Human Nature, Penguin, London, 1984; R. C. Lewontin, *Biology as Ideology: The Doctrine of DNA*, HarperCollins, New York, 1991.

58 See C. Rovirosa-Madrazo, *La caída del estado y el advenimiento de la 'genetocracia'* (forthcoming, 2009), and C. Rovirosa-Madrazo, 'De aborto, guerra, genética y poder', Universal Forum of Cultures, Monterrey, 2007. Concerning general issues of genome patenting and 'biopiracy', see Lander, 'Eurocentrism, modern knowledges'. For a more general discussion, see Matthew Rimmer, 'The genographic project: traditional knowledge and population genetics', *Australian Indigenous Law Review*, vol. 11, no. 2 (2007): 33–54; see also the work of Harvard Professor, geneticist and philosopher of science, Richard Lewontin, *It Ain't Necessarily So: The Dream of the Human Genome and Other Illusions*, New York Review Books, New York, 2000; Lewontin, *Biology as Ideology*.

59 See particularly the Declaracion sobre la Ciencia y la Utilizacion del Conocimiento Cientifico, UNESCO, Conferencia Mundial sobre Ciencia, Budapest, 1999, and the Universal Declaration on the Human Genome and Human Rights, adopted unanimously and by acclamation at UNESCO's 29th General Conference on 11 Nov. 1997.

60 M. S. Dominguez, 'Una nueva biología para una nueva sociedad', *Política y Sociedad*, vol. 39, no. 3 (2002).

61 Z. Bauman, *Society under Siege*, Polity, Cambridge, 2002; Z. Bauman, 'Power and insecurity: a genealogy of "official fear"', *Esprit*, no. 11 (2003): 39–48.

Conversation I

1 Towards the end of 2009 governments will meet again in Copenhagen at what is considered by some non-governmental organizations to be the most important meeting ever aimed at saving the planet, as a new strategy to replace the Kyoto Protocol will be agreed.

2 See, on this issue, 'Growing fuel: the wrong way, the right way', *National Geographic* (Oct. 2007). For a very different perspective on biofuels, see *New Internationalist*, no. 419 (Jan. 2009), at www.newint.org/features/2009/01/01/keynote-climate-justice/.

3 After his mandate ended, former Mexican president Luis Echeverria Álvarez created and directed the internationally renowned Centre for Economic and Social Studies of the Third World. This was part of an interview conducted for an ongoing research project regarding foreign policy and the impact worldwide of the so-called third world movement.

4 See Kay Glans and Johanna Laurin (eds), *Towards an Hourglass Society?* Glasshouse Forum, Stockholm, 2008, pp. 24–6.

Conversation II

1 More recently, in 2008, Bauman discussed the issue in his address to the Joseph Rowntree Foundation at the forum on Exploring Twenty-First Century Social Evils, York.
2 Z. Bauman, *Wasted Lives: Modernity and its Outcasts*, Polity, Cambridge, 2003.
3 Bauman, *Postmodernity and its Discontents*, pp. 35–45.
4 Ibid., p. 44.
5 See Oliver James, 'Selfish capitalism is bad for our mental health', *Guardian*, 3 Jan. 2008.

Conversation III

1 See Rovirosa-Madrazo, 'Indigenous rights'.
2 Bauman, *Socialism*.
3 Michel Houellebecq, *The Possibility of an Island*, trans. Gavin Bowd, Phoenix, London, 2006.
4 Samuel Beckett, *Texts for Nothing*, John Calder, London, 1999, pp. 23, 20, 32.
5 Miguel Abensour, 'Persistent utopia', *Constellations*, vol. 15, no. 3 (Sept. 2008): 406–21.
6 William Morris, *A Dream of John Ball; and, a king's lesson*, available electronically from Project Gutenberg at www.gutenberg.org.
7 Ernst Bloch, *The Principle of Hope*, MIT Press, Cambridge, 1995, p. 306.
8 See Russell Jacoby, *Picture Imperfect: Utopian Thought for an Anti-utopian Age*, Columbia University Press, New York, 2005, pp. xiv–xv.
9 Z. Bauman, 'The rise and fall of labour', *Sotsiologicheskie Issledovaniya*, vol. 5 (2004): 77–86.
10 C. Rovirosa-Madrazo, 'This thing post-modern Zapatismo: ethnocentrism and ethnic conflict in Mexico', roundtable discussion on Indigenous Perspectives on the Mexican Nation-State, Latin American Centre, Essex University, 16 June 1994; see also Rovirosa-Madrazo, 'Indigenous rights'.
11 C. Rovirosa-Madrazo, 'Chiapas: from bellum justum to XXI century constitutional narratives', paper delivered at the international conference 'Peace Building in Chiapas', University of York, 9 July 2002.

12 L. Villoro, 'Otra vision del mundo (II)', *La Jornada*, 18 Jan. 2009.
13 At www.counterpunch.org/giroux02062009.html.
14 Sheldon Wolin, *Democracy, Inc.: Managed Democracy and the Specter of Inverted Totalitarianism*, Princeton University Press, Princeton, 2008, pp. 260–1.
15 Jerry Z. Muller, 'Us and them: the enduring power of ethnic nationalism', *Foreign Affairs* vol. 87, no. 2 (Mar.–Apr. 2008).
16 G. O'Donnell et al., *La democracia en America Latina. Hacia una democracia de ciudadanos y ciudadanas*, United Nations Development Programme, New York, 2004.
17 On logocentrism as ethnocentrism and the state, see Rovirosa-Madrazo, 'Indigenous rights', pp. 81–97; Rovirosa-Madrazo, 'Analfabetismens censur'. See, for the case in point, W. G. F. Hegel, *Philosophy of Subjective Spirit*, vol. 3: *Phenomenology and Psychology*, ed. and trans. M. J. Perry, Reidel, Dordrecht, 1978, p. 187, §§ 5–20; W. G. F. Hegel, *Philosophy of Right*, trans. T. M. Knox, Oxford University Press, Oxford, 1967, p. 130, §§ 215, 111.
18 In a recent interview published by the Spanish newspaper *La Vanguardia* and partially reproduced in the *Daily Telegraph*.
19 C. Rovirosa-Madrazo, *Pueblos indigenas: soberania o autodeterminacion. La batalla de paradigmas en la era del NeoZapatismo y el advenimiento indigena en America Latina* (forthcoming 2009)
20 Bauman, *Consuming Life*, Polity, Cambridge, 2007, pp. 62–7.
21 The idea of 'sovereignty' stemming from 'the Divine' was skilfully and cunningly developed by the European colonial powers – the Spanish Catholic Crown being of great historical significance because it developed its empire in American territories on a concept of sovereignty based on the idea of *bellum justum* ('just war') over indigenous lands overseas, as an authority and dictum coming from God Himself (see Rovirosa-Madrazo, 'Indigenous rights').
22 Bauman, *Consuming Life*, p. 65.
23 Carl Schmitt, *Political Theology*, trans. George Schwab from *Politische Theologie: Vier Kapitel zur Lehre von der Souveränität* (1922), University of Chicago Press, Chicago, 1985, pp. 36, 10.
24 Carl Schmitt, *Theorie des Partisanen, Zwischenbemerkung zum Begriff des Politischen*, Duncker & Humboldt, Berlin, 1963, p. 80. See the discussion in Giorgio Agamben, *Homo Sacer: Sovereign Power and Bare Life*, trans. Daniel Heller-Roazen, Stanford University Press, Stanford, 1998, p. 137.
25 Schmitt, *Political Theology*, pp. 19–21, italics added; see discussion in Agamben, *Homo Sacer*, pp. 15 ff.
26 Agamben, *Homo Sacer*, p. 18, italics added.

27 Ernst-Wolfgang Böckenförde, *Recht, Staat, Freiheit*, Suhrkamp, Frankfurt, 1991, p. 112.
28 See Jan-Werner Müller, *A Dangerous Mind: Carl Schmitt in Post-war European Thought*, Yale University Press, New Haven, 2003, pp. 4–5.
29 Schmitt, *Political Theology*, p. 37.
30 Ibid., p. 48.
31 Carl Schmitt, *The Concept of the Political*, trans. George Schwab from *Der Begriff des Politischen*, University of Chicago Press, Chicago, 2007, p. 26.
32 Ibid., p. 27.
33 See Ulrich Beck, *Risk Society*, trans Mark Ritter, Sage, London, 1992, p. 137.
34 On the Eurocentric foundations and general history of the League of Nations, see J. E. Falkowski, *Indian Law/Race Law: A Five Hundred-Year History*, Praeger, New York, 1992. See also Rovirosa-Madrazo, 'Indigenous rights'; G. Schwarzenberger, *Power Politics: A Study of World Society*, Stevens & Sons, London, 1964. Regarding the specific relevant provisions, see the Non-Self Governing Territories Provision and the 1960 Declaration Regarding the Granting of Independence to Colonial Peoples.
35 Adopted by General Assembly Resolution 61/295, 13 Sept. 2007.
36 See C. Douzinas, *Human Rights and Empire: The Political Philosophy of Cosmopolitanism*, Routledge-Cavendish, London, 2007.
37 C. Rovirosa-Madrazo, 'Objetivos de desarrollo del milenio y derechos indígenas. Apuntes para una estrategia pedagógica de transgresión epistemológica en la educación para los derechos humanos', paper delivered at the Universal Forum of Cultures, Monterrey, 2007; Rovirosa-Madrazo, 'Analfabetismens censur'.
38 This includes the change from a discourse focused on *civil and political rights* to one focused on *social and economic rights* and beyond. For a review of the different currents, see R. K. Smith and C. van den Anker, *The Essentials of Human Rights*, Hodder Arnold, New York, 2005. For a critical approach, see Douzinas, *Human Rights and Empire*; C. Douzinas, *The End of Human Rights: Critical Legal Thought at the Fin-de-Siecle*, Hart, Oxford, 2000; and S. Zizek, *The Obscenity of Human Rights: Violence as Symptom* (2005), at www.lacan.com/zizviol.htm. For a further discussion, see Rovirosa-Madrazo, 'Objetivos de desarrollo' and, for a more recent debate regarding the 'indeterminacy' of 'the universal', see J. Butler, 'Restaging the universal: hegemony and the limits of formalism' and S. Zizek, 'Holding the place', both in J. Butler, E. Laclau and

S. Zizek, *Contingency, Hegemony, Universality*, Verso, London, 2000.

39 See the Barcelona Declaration of Emerging Human Rights.

40 See H. Bellinghausen, 'La invención del miedo', *La Jornada*, 15 Sept. 2008, and P. Sloterdijk, *Temblores de aire, en las fuentes del terror*, Pre-Textos, Valencia, 2003; see also A. Vásquez Rocca, 'Peter Sloterdijk. Temblores de aire, atmoterrorismo y crepúsculo de la inmunidad', *Nomadas, Revista Crítica de Ciencias Sociales y Jurídicas* (Universidad Complutense de Madrid), no. 17 (2008): 159–70.

41 Thus, in recent statements, lawyers from the Geneva-based International Commission of Jurists, led by former United Nations High Commissioner for Human Rights Mary Robinson, warned of the long-term damage done to civil liberties since the terrorist attacks of 9/11.

42 M. Weber, *The Theory of Social and Economic Organization*, Free Press, New York, 1964.

43 See *La Jornada*, 13 Nov. 2009.

Conversation IV

1 Elliot, *The Contemporary Bauman*.

2 Bauman, *Modernity and the Holocaust*, p. 87.

3 Bauman, *Conversations with Keith Tester*, p. 91.

4 Particularly the Convention for the Prevention and Punishment of the Crime of Genocide.

5 W. Schabas, 'Freedom from genocide', in Smith and van den Anker, *The Essentials of Human Rights*, p. 141.

6 L. Kuper, *Genocide: Its Political Use in the Twentieth Century*, Yale University Press, New Haven, 1982.

7 The case of the indigenous nations in Latin America is compelling. The numbers of indigenous organizations that claim to be at risk of genocide and extermination across the American continent is not to be underestimated. Genocidal actions are said to range from mass sterilization of indigenous people, to land occupation and forced displacement. Thus, according to the BBC, in 2003 a Peruvian parliamentary commission reopened an investigation into the forced sterilization of more than 300,000 indigenous Peruvian women allegedly authorized by former president Alberto Fujimori. Peru's Human Rights Commission claims mass sterilizations were carried out negligently between 1995 and 2000 (see BBC, 18 June 2003, at http://news.bbc.co.uk/go/pr/fr/-/1/hi/world/americas/3000454.stm).

8 See Ian Kershaw, *Fateful Choices*, Penguin, London, 2007, p. 436.

Conversation V

1   Bauman, *Liquid Love*; Bauman, *Identity*.

2   See on this issue Dominguez, 'Una nueva biologia'; M. S. Dominguez, 'En busca de la biología. Reflexiones sobre la evolución' (2009), at www.iieh.com/Evolucion/articulos_evolucion47.php. See also Lewontin, *Biology as Ideology*; Lewontin, *It Ain't Necessarily So*; and R. C. Lewontin, *The Triple Helix: Gene, Organism and Environment*, Harvard University Press, Cambridge, 2004. Also J. Muñoz Rubio, 'La ética socio-biológica. Ideología de la enajenación humana', *Ludus Vitalis*, vol. 19, no. 26 (2006): 251–4; and J. Muñoz Rubio, 'On Darwinian discourses: anthropologization of nature in the naturalization of man', *Human Nature Review* (2005), at www.human-nature.com/science-as-culture/julio.html.

3   Bauman, *Modernity and the Holocaust*, pp. 66–72.

4   On this issue see the excellent paper by Dominguez, 'Una nueva biologia', and Dominguez, 'En busca de la biología'. See also Lewontin, *Biology as Ideology*; Lewontin, *It Ain't Necessarily So*; Lewontin, *The Triple Helix*.

5   Julian Huxley, *Man in the Modern World*, Chatto & Windus, London, 1947, p. 22. On the same issue and Huxley's position on eugenics, see ibid., pp. 22–55. See also Elazar Barkan, *The Retreat of Scientific Racism: Changing Concepts of Race in Britain and the United States between the World Wars*, Cambridge University Press, New York, 1999; and John P. Jackson Jr and Nadine M. Weidman (eds), *Race, Racism and Science: Social Impact and Interaction*, Rutgers University Press, New Brunswick, 2005. This book refers extensively to Huxley's inclination for eugenics (p. 157), including the fact that Huxley was among those who considered sterilization (p. 187). See also the following sources (quoted in Jackson and Weidman, *Race, Racism and Science*): J. Huxley, 'The vital importance of eugenics', letter to the Editor, 'Nature and nurture', *New Leader*, 29 Feb. 1924; J. Huxley, 'Eugenics and heredity', letter to the Editor, *New Statesman*, 1924.

6   On contrasting perspectives regarding debates on unlimited growth and finite natural resources, see the work of Angus Maddison, Professor Emeritus of Economic Growth and Development at the University of Groningen, who has written about the history of economic growth and noted that population growth follows the same trend as economic growth. See also the works of the winner of the Nobel Memorial Prize in Economic Sciences (1998): Amartya Sen, *Poverty and Famines: An Essay on Entitlement and Deprivation*, Oxford University Press, Oxford, 1981. In contrast to the latter, the Club

of Rome blames the increase in food prices on the demands of a growing population in developing countries. Eberhard von Koeber, co-president of the Club of Rome, insisted at a recent meeting in London of Globe International: 'Unlimited growth on a planet with finite resources cannot go on forever' (BBC, 21 Jan. 2009). It has been noted against this argument that there is a growing demand for biofuels, with the US subsidizing ethanol production and diverting corn crops from food to fuel (which reduces supply and hence increases price as demand grows).

7 In 2000, 189 member states of the UN gathered in New York at what was considered the most transcendental UN summit ever to face the challenges of world poverty. The Millennium Declaration adopted at the UN Millennium Summit (Sept. 2000) contained the so-called Millennium Development Goals (MDGs) or targets to be achieved by 2015 in order to reduce world poverty. The MDGs, which are broken down into 21 quantifiable targets that are measured by several indicators, are the following: (1) Eradicate extreme poverty and hunger; (2) Achieve universal primary education; (3) Promote gender equality and empower women; (4) Reduce child mortality; (5) Improve maternal health; (6) Combat HIV/AIDS, malaria and other diseases; (7) Ensure environmental sustainability; (8) Develop a global partnership for development. See www.unmillenniumproject.org.

8 It is important to recall that the IMF was founded in the wake of the 'Great Depression' of the 1930s, after which an international framework of international economic cooperation was designed, in 1945, to tackle the economic crisis.

9 See M. Murray and G. King, 'The effects of International Monetary Fund loans on health outcomes' (2008), at www.plosmedicine.org/article/info:doi/10.1371/journal.pmed.0050162; and D. Stuckler, L. P. King and S. Basu, 'International Monetary Fund programs and tuberculosis outcomes in post-communist countries' (2008), at www.plosmedicine.org/article/info:doi/10.1371/journal.pmed.0050143.

10 See *Report of the TUC*, Sixteenth Annual Trades Union Congress, Nottingham, 10–15 Sept. 1883, Co-operative Printing Society, Manchester, 1883, p. 89.

11 Quoted from J. B. Jeffreys, *Labour's Formative Years*, Lawrence & Wishart, London, 1948.

12 See Jacques Donzelot, Catherine Mével and Anne Wyvekens, 'De la fabrique sociale aux violences urbaines', *Esprit* (Dec. 2002): 13–34.

13 See David Maybury-Lewis, 'Genocide against indigenous peoples', in Alexander Laban Hinton (ed.), *Annihilating Difference: The*

Anthropology of Genocide, University of California Press, Berkeley, 2002, pp. 43–53.

14 Quoted from Herman Merivale, *Lectures on Colonization and Colonies*, Green, Longman & Roberts, London, 1861, p. 541.

15 Theodore Roosevelt, *The Winning of the West: From the Alleghanies to the Mississippi, 1769–1776*, G. P. Putnam's Sons, New York, 1889, p. 90.

16 According to Alfredo M. Serres Güiraldes, *La Estrategia de General Roca*, Pleamar, Buenos Aires, 1979, pp. 377–8, quoted by Merivale, *Lectures on Colonization and Colonies*.

17 At www.dieoff.org/page27.htm. In *Le Monde*, 28 Nov. 2008, in a brief article celebrating the hundredth anniversary of the great anthropologist and founder of structural anthropology, Claude Lévi-Strauss, I found the following information. 'The world I knew, the world I loved, had 2.5 billion inhabitants,' Lévi-Strauss had told *Le Monde* three years earlier. In his opinion, now, however, the destruction of vegetable and animal species, the staggering demographic prospect (of 9 billion humans) is poisoning the future and casts 'the human species . . . in a kind of "internal poisoning" condition'. It seems that this worry filled the final stages of his long life dedicated to piercing through the mysteries of the human way of being-in-the-world, and the twisted logic of that way's history. Lévi-Strauss seems to have watched – from aside, haplessly and resignedly, not knowing what could be done to avert the imminent catastrophe – as, having broken one after the other most of the constraints imposed by Nature on their proliferation, humans stumbled towards the destiny of being the prime victim of their own triumph, drawing to destruction the Nature they had doggedly fought and joyously conquered. There are currently many objectives at which human actions, undertaken singly or collectively, are aimed – but, except for the Chinese enforcement of the 'one child per family' policy, restriction of total population numbers does *not* figure among them. Demographic trends are not determined in advance by any agency with a final number of humans in mind; the science of demography is a guessing game, and its prognoses have thus far systematically failed to be verified by the course of events; little if anything augurs that under present conditions their credibility may improve. The actual trends are now, as throughout human history, the combined effects and sediments of a multitude of mutually unconnected and uncoordinated decisions and/or 'occurrences' that no one decided to make occur (variously called 'blows of fate', 'finger of providence', the 'invisible hand of the markets', or left nameless for absence of a plausible rhetorical figure). Single, sepa-

rate and disparate actions may be planned, but their summary, wholesale effects hardly ever are and obstinately elude prediction. To make things yet more confusing, whatever inchoate attempts are sporadically made to reflect on the 'limited sustainability of the Earth' or the ecologically destructive long-term side-effects of rampant and chaotic urbanization and untidy and wasteful planet-polluting consumption, and however earnest the intentions some-times are to do something to mitigate them – the practical results of such reflections and intentions are more than counterbalanced and cancelled by the thought and money invested (whether with morally commendable or immoral intentions) in fighting and con-quering the immediate harms done by those long-term processes: finding new sources of fuel to burn, plugging the transitory holes in consumer demand, inventing new genuinely or putatively effec-tive technologies to stretch life's longevity, and dealing with ad hoc concerns about local condensations of damage that are outstanding, spectacular and particularly offensive to the public conscience.

18 See on this issue J. Jenson, H. Elisabeth and C. Reddy, *Feminization of the Labour Force*, Polity, Cambridge, 1988.

19 In 2007, news was made public that US government officials of the Food and Drug Administration (FDA) had approved the commer-cialization of a pill that would indefinitely suppress the menstrual period (Reuters, 23 May 2007). During the same period, motivated by medical research and urged on by the long-term treatment of the future fertility of a minor with cancer, scientists at the University of Hadassah in Israel ventured to isolate eggs in a five-year-old girl (*Daily Telegraph*, 2 July 2007), thus opening up serious moral debates regarding the reproductive future of an entire generation of girls. The creation of an artificial uterus is no longer a fantasy: for scientists at Tokyo University this has become a reality; in their view, their artificial uterus 'will offer better and more comfortable conditions for the embryo than the biological uterus' (*New Scientist*, 27 July 2007).

20 In Mattopoisset, the creation of Marge Piercy in *Woman at the Edge of Time* (Fawcett, 1977), Connie, a Mexican-American woman who has travelled in time after experiencing rape and racial discrimina-tion, and who has lost custody of her daughter, soon realizes that motherhood has been abolished. In Mattopoisset gender is forever eliminated. Babies are artificially conceived through random genetic selection, and are developed in an artificial uterus. But all is not well for Connie in the promised land of degendered motherhood.

21 In her *The Dialectics of Sex* (Women's Press, London, 1979) S. Firestone proposed a 'biological' interpretation of Marxism and

invoked a 'revolution in the *re-productive forces*'. Firestone's work contributed to a tradition of radical feminism known for its challenging and belligerent attacks on motherhood.

22   Dominguez, 'Una nueva biologia', p. 68.

23   G. Corea, *The Mother Machine: Reproductive Technologies from Artificial Insemination to Artificial Wombs*, Harper & Row, New York, 1985.

24   Please note that these observations are not intended to pass judgement on IVF.

25   Thus Rosemary Tong refers to feminists who have argued that 'reproductive technologies posed an enormous threat to whatever little powers women still possessed and that biological reproduction ought not to be forsaken in favor of artificial motherhood': Rosemary Tong, *Feminist Thought: A Comprehensive Introduction*, Routledge, London, 1994, p. 81.

26   In addition to the previously mentioned biotechnical experimentations, another relevant development in the field of artificial intelligence is that of the rapid spread of the 'robots industry', which has designed and commercialized new robots to look after children. Over a dozen companies based in South Korea and Japan manufacture, on an increasingly industrial scale, robot 'companions' and 'carers' with the potential to gradually replace the 'traditional role of mothers'. Professor Noel Sharkey from Sheffield University, observing that 'these robots now are so safe that parents can leave their children with them for hours, or even days', warns that children could be left without human contact for long periods; to him it is a concern that 'the psychological impact of the varying degrees of social isolation on development is unknown' (*Independent*, 19 Dec. 2008). It is ironic that this industry is also involved in the production of lethal robots which, Sharkey explains, were deployed in Iraq and Afghanistan.

27   Though, of course, this might crystallize, if at all, only in decades or centuries to come . . .

28   Houellebecq, *The Possibility of an Island*, p. 388.

Conversation VI

1   For the sake of openness, I thought I should clarify that I see myself as Christian – perhaps classed by some as some kind of 'dissident' and certainly not 'a good Christian', or perhaps even guilty of 'heresy'.

2   N. Machiavelli, *The Prince*, Modern Library, New York, 1940; E. Cassirer, *The Myth of the State*, Yale University Press, New Haven, 1961, p. 138.

3   Bauman, *Identity*, p. 72.
4   Ibid., p. 73.
5   Ibid., p. 75.
6   U. Eco, *A paso de Cangrego. Articulos, reflexiones y decepciones*, Debate Ensayos, Madrid, 2006, pp. 284–7.
7   Roberto Toscano and Ramin Jahanbegloo, *Beyond Violence: Principles for an Open Century*, Har-Anand, New Delhi, 2009, p. 78. On the issue of child slavery and child prostitution, see Christian van den Anker (ed.), *The Political Economy of New Slavery*, Palgrave Macmillan, London.
8   Bauman, *The Absence of Society*, p. 7.
9   Bauman, *Conversations with Keith Tester*, p. 134.
10 Eco, *A paso de Cangrejo*, p. 287.
11 A reference to Richard Dawkins. See also J. R. Brown.
12 Z. Bauman, *The Art of Life*, Polity, Cambridge, 2008.
13 Lawrence Grossberg, 'Affect and postmodernity in the struggle over "American modernity"', in Pelagia Goulimari (ed.), *Postmodernism: What Moment?* Manchester University Press, Manchester, 2007, pp. 176–201.

Conversation VII

1   As a matter of clarification, I am not sure I would be inclined to speak of 'scientific fundamentalism' – rather I would prefer to speak of dogmatic interpretations of scientific knowledge (cf. P. Feyerabend, *Farewell to Reason*, Verso, London, 1987, and P. Feyerabend, *Against Method*, Verso, London, 1988). See also T. Kuhn, *The Structure of Scientific Revolutions*, University of Chicago Press, Chicago, 1970.
2   On the issue of geoengineering for climate change, see the Royal Society Working Group on Geoengineering, at http://royalsociety. org/page.asp?tip=1&id=8086. Regarding a campaign for governance on the matter, see www.etcgroup.org/en/issues/geoengineering. html. On issues of genetically modified food and organisms, see J. Muñoz Rubio (ed.), *Alimentos transgénicos, ciencia, ambiente y mercado. Un debate abierto*, Siglo XXI, Mexico City, 2004. See also J. Muñoz Rubio, 'Transgénicos. Biología desde el reduccionismo', *Revista Digital Universitaria*, vol. 10, no. 4 (Apr. 2009).
3   James Watson, Nobel Prize for Science (1962) for his findings on DNA.
4   *Guardian*, 6 Oct. 2007.
5   See Rovirosa-Madrazo, *La caída del estado*, and Rovirosa-Madrazo, 'De aborto, guerra, genetica y poder'.

6   On the defence of the Genographic Project (GP) and its ethical framework, see https://genographic.nationalgeographic.com/geno-graphic/index.html. Regarding the objection by the indigenous peoples to the GP and, before it, the so-called Human Genome Diversity Project, see M. Dodson and R. Williamson, 'Indigenous peoples and the Human Genome Diversity Project', *Journal of Medical Ethics*, vol. 24 (1999): 204–8. On these issues, see www.ipcb.org/issues/human_genetics, and on the common argument that scientists want to 'colonize and exploit indigenous bodies', see the statements by the International Indian Treaty Council at www.treatycouncil.org/section_2117331.htm. Here the International Indian Treaty Council claims that the Genographic Project is 'exploitive and unethical research that undermines indigenous rights'. The council objected: 'They will tell you who you are and where you come from, ignoring existing Indigenous knowledge about ourselves.' It is important to observe that the informed consent form issued by the GP states: 'It is possible that some of findings that result from this study may contradict an oral, written, or other traditional knowledge held by you or by members of your group . . .'. On this particular issue, see also Rimmer, 'The genographic project'. Jenny Reardon's book *Race to the Finish: Identity and Governance in an Age of Genomics*, Princeton University Press, Princeton, 2005, focuses on the history of the Human Genome Diversity Project, its complexity and the controversy surrounding it. For an academic discussion on genomics and geography, see the series of reports by the Economic and Social Research Council's Genomic Policy and Research Forum, including 'Classifying genomics: how social categories shape scientific and medical practice; with special focus on race and ethnicity', pdf available at www.genomicsforum.ac.uk. See also 'The race myth: more sincere fictions in the age of genomics', report on a public lecture by Dr Joseph L. Graves, Oct. 2006, in pdf at the same site. In this report by the ESRC Forum, the work of Joseph L. Graves and his distinction between 'biological and geographical populations' and 'races' is widely discussed. For a more lengthy discussion on this matter, see also Joseph L. Graves, *The Emperor's New Clothes: Biological Theories of Race at the Millennium*, Rutgers University Press, New Brunswick, 2002.

7   On the issue of so-called biopiracy, see www.etcgroup.org/en/issues/biopiracy.html. On this website, belonging to a non-profit international organization based in Canada, 'biopiracy' is defined as 'the appropriation of the knowledge and genetic resources of farming and indigenous communities by individuals or institutions who seek exclusive monopoly control (patents or intellectual property) over

these resources and knowledge. ETC group believes that intellectual property is predatory on the rights and knowledge of farming communities and indigenous peoples.'

8 The more recent shifts in the focus of scientific and technological research from broad controversial areas (such as nuclear research) in the twentieth century, to DNA, stem cells and research in genetically modified food and organisms more recently, have also represented a shift in the relationship of the scientific community with the political community and the market.

9 See, on this issue, D. Alexander, *Rebuilding the Matrix: Science and Faith in the Twenty-First Century*, Lion, Oxford, 2001.

10 Bauman, *Identity*, p. 72.

11 See www.newscientist.com/article/mg18524911.600-13-things-that-do-not-make-sense.html.

12 R. Feynman, *The Character of Physical Law*, a series of lectures at Cornell University recorded by the BBC, Cox & Wyman, London, 1962.

13 In an article by Silvia Ribeiro published in *La Jornada* (8 Nov. 2008), nanotechnology is described as having played 'a crucial role in capitalist regeneration' during the last decade. It involves the manipulation of matter at the atomic and molecular levels. It is the platform for industrial innovation and is essential for areas such as genomics, biotechnology, the pharmaceutical industry, agriculture and the fuel industries. 'Some organizations', explains Ribeiro, 'speak of over 700 products in the market depending on nanotech applications, with a fourth of the pharmaceutical industry depending on it. All patents are monopolies of transnational corporations such as IBM, DuPont, Hitachi, Procter & Gamble, as well as the armies in the US and the EU and universities which, funded with public money, are known to have granted licensing to international corporations' (ibid.). However, Koïchiro Matsuura, Director-General of UNESCO, has optimistic views of the potential of such technologies and great expectations not only for development, but for ecological preservation. The debate is not over.

14 See Brown, *Who Rules in Science?*

15 An equivalent metaphor was used about developments in biology regarding mother cells in referring to the 'Holy Grail' when scientists recently made further progress on stem cell research, revealing the parallelism of scientific and religious metaphors.

16 In 1996, the cultural studies journal *Social Text* published a paper with the title 'Transgressing the boundaries: toward a transformative hermeneutics of quantum gravity'. It turned out to be nothing less than a hoax! In his defence, Sokal argued that he

was trying to demonstrate that academics in the social sciences working in the context of postmodernism were making serious epistemological mistakes in their perception of scientific knowledge. Claims such as 'laws of physics are mere social conventions' are, he argued in his most recent book, *Beyond the Hoax*, an example of the dimension of epistemological mistakes. As Robert Matthews puts it in his review of Sokal's last book in the *Times Higher Education Supplement* (13 Mar. 2008), Sokal is aiming to stress his fear that academics on the left have become vulnerable to relativist philosophies. In his view, such an approach threatens to undermine their critique of the structure of society: 'if there is no "truth" but merely "claims of truth", how can the Left hope to win the debate over its adversaries?'.

Conversation VIII

1 Bauman, *Identity*, pp. 62–5.
2 See Michel Foucault, *The History of Sexuality*, vol. 1, trans. Robert Hurley, Penguin, London, 1978, pp. 42 ff.
3 See 'Les victimes de violences sexuelles en parlent de plus en plus', *Le Monde*, 30 May 2008.
4 Frank Furedi, 'Thou shalt not hug', *New Statesman*, 26 June 2008.
5 See Richard Wray, 'How one year's digital output would fill 161bn iPods', *Guardian*, 6 March 2007.

Index